Indigenous Peoples and the Human Rights-Based Approach to Development: Engaging in Dialogue

Cordillera Indigenous Peoples' Legal Centre (DINTEG) and UNDP Regional Initiative on Indigenous Peoples' Rights and Development (RIPP)

The authors are responsible for the facts contained in their papers, and for the opinions expressed therein, which do not necessarily represent the view of the United Nations Development Programme (UNDP) or commit UNDP in any way.

Cover photograph: Helen M. Leake
Inside photographs contributed by Colin Nicholas and Raja Devasish Roy

Design and layout: Keen Publishing (Thailand) Co., Ltd.

Copyright © 2007

United Nations Development Programme
Regional Centre in Bangkok: Serving Asia and the Pacific
3rd Floor, UN Service Building
Rajdamnern Nok Avenue, Bangkok, Thailand
Tel: +66 (2) 288 2470, Fax: +66 (2) 280 2700
Website: http://regionalcentrebangkok.undp.or.th

ISBN: 978-92-1-126205-6

Preface

In Asia Pacific, indigenous peoples continue to be disproportionately represented in the poorest and most vulnerable sections of society, experiencing a history of discrimination and marginalization. Despite years of indigenous advocacy – with many positive outcomes – this situation continues to worsen in many countries. Strong economic growth in the majority of Asian countries has failed to bring significant benefits for indigenous peoples, and indeed levels of poverty and dispossession from lands and resources are rising. Development has further exacerbated this situation in many countries, with the appropriation of indigenous lands for development purposes, and large-scale plantation and forestry projects a major contributor.

The United Nations Development Programme (UNDP) has responded to the challenges facing indigenous peoples in the Asia Pacific region with the establishment of a regional initiative on indigenous peoples' rights and development. The aim of the programme is to facilitate dialogue and strengthen the framework for regional cooperation. To this end, this initiative, the Regional Indigenous Peoples' Programme (RIPP), works with a range of sectors to promote the recognition and protection of indigenous peoples' rights. UNDP has a unique role in assisting indigenous peoples, as recognized by the Policy of Engagement, UNDP's policy statement on indigenous peoples:

> *UNDP's coordinating role at the country level, its human development paradigm, advocacy of democratic governance, and policy of mainstreaming human rights positions makes it a key partner for pursuing a more holistic approach to development. Moreover, UNDP's country presence and the relationship of trust it has with governments and civil society partners enable UNDP to play a unique role in bringing together different stakeholders in development processes.*

UNDP Policy of Engagement with Indigenous Peoples, 2001

The fundamental link between human rights and development implicit in this policy of engagement was also affirmed in 2000 in the Millennium Declaration and the associated Millennium Development Goals (MDGs). The Declaration states: "We will spare no effort to promote democracy and strengthen the rule of law, as well as respect for all internationally recognized human rights and fundamental freedoms, including the right to development." This link between human rights and development articulated in the Millennium Declaration underpins and frames all development work undertaken by the United Nations.

UNDP, in collaboration with other UN agencies, seeks to meet this challenge though advocating and using a human rights-based approach to development. Simply put, this entails the promotion and protection of human rights not only in the outcome of projects and programmes, but in the methods through which projects and programmes are implemented. The right to participation, the right to self-determination and the right to development are implicit in this approach.

This publication reflects this approach to development, seeking to examine the development policies of agencies and organizations from a human rights-based perspective. It represents a step in a dialogue process in which key development financing institutions are engaging with indigenous peoples' organizations and representatives to better enable rights-based design and implementation of development initiatives. UNDP would like to thank the Indigenous Peoples' Legal Centre (DINTEG) in the Philippines for taking the lead in making this process of dialogue a reality. We would also like to thank all the authors who have contributed to the analysis in this publication.

We hope that this publication assists international development financing institutions in their engagement with indigenous peoples on national, regional and global levels. It is also hoped that this publication will serve as a tool for indigenous peoples in advocating for their rights in development processes that impact them. UNDP is committed to the realization of indigenous peoples' rights in Asia Pacific and to partnering with international development agencies, governments and indigenous peoples.

Chandra Roy
Regional Coordinator
Regional Initiative on Indigenous Peoples' Rights and Development
Regional Centre in Bangkok
United Nations Development Programme

Contents

Acronyms

ADB	Asian Development Bank
AWIN	Asian Indigenous Women's Network
CAFGU	Civilian Armed Forces Geographical Unit (Philippines)
CAMC	Climax Arimco Mining Company (Philippines)
CPA	Cordillera Peoples' Alliance (Philippines)
CPPAP	Conservation of Priority Protected Areas Project
CHARM	Cordillera Highland Agricultural Resource Management (Philippines)
CHT	Chittagong Hill Tracts (Bangladesh)
COAC	Centre for Orang Asli Concerns (Malaysia)
CSO	civil society organization
CWERC	Cordillera Women's Education and Resource Centre (Philippines)
DCM	developing country member (Asian Development Bank)
DINTEG	Cordillera Indigenous Peoples Legal Centre (Philippines), DINTEG is an indigenous term for 'law and justice'
EBRD	European Bank for Reconstruction and Development
EC	European Commission
ECA	export credit agencies
EI	extractive industries
EIR	Extractive Industries Review
ESIA	environmental and social impact assessment
FPIC	free prior and informed consent
FPICon	free prior and informed consultation
FTAA	Financial and Technical Assistance Agreement
HRBA	human rights-based approach
HURIST	Human Rights Strengthening (a joint programme between UNDP and OHCHR)
IAITPTF	International Alliance of Indigenous and Tribal Peoples of Tropical Forests
IASG	Inter-Agency Support Group
IBRD	International Bank for Reconstruction and Development (part of World Bank Group)

ICERD	International Convention on the Elimination of All Forms of Racial Discrimination
ICSID	International Center for Settlement of Investment Disputes (part of World Bank Group)
IDA	International Development Association (part of World Bank Group)
IFC	International Finance Corporation (part of World Bank Group)
IFI	international financial institution
IFO	international financial operation
ILO	International Labour Organization
IMF	International Monetary Fund
IP	indigenous peoples
IPO	indigenous peoples organization
IPP	Indigenous Peoples Plan (World Bank Group)
IPPF	Indigenous Peoples Plan Framework (World Bank Group)
IPRA	Indigenous Peoples' Rights Act (Philippines)
JBIC	Japan Bank for International Cooperation
JEXIM	Japan Export-Import Bank
JICA	Japan International Cooperation Agency
MIGA	Multilateral Investment Guarantee Agency (part of World Bank Group)
MDG	Millennium Development Goal
NGO	non-government organization
ODA	official development assistance
OECD	Organization of Economic Cooperation and Development
OECF	Overseas Economic Cooperation Fund
OD	Operation Directive (World Bank Group)
OHCHR	Office of the United Nations High Commissioner for Human Rights
OMS	Operational Manual Statement (World Bank Group)
OP	Operational Policy (World Bank Group)
PFII	Permanent Forum on Indigenous Issues (United Nations)

PRSP	Poverty Reduction Strategy Paper
PS	performance standard (World Bank Group)
RCB	Regional Centre in Bangkok (United Nations Development Programme)
RIPP	Regional Initiative on Indigenous Peoples' Rights and Development
TEPSCO	Tokyo Electric Power Services Co., Ltd
UN	United Nations
UNDP	United Nations Development Programme
WB	World Bank
WBG	World Bank Group
WCD	World Commission on Dams
WTO	World Trade Organization

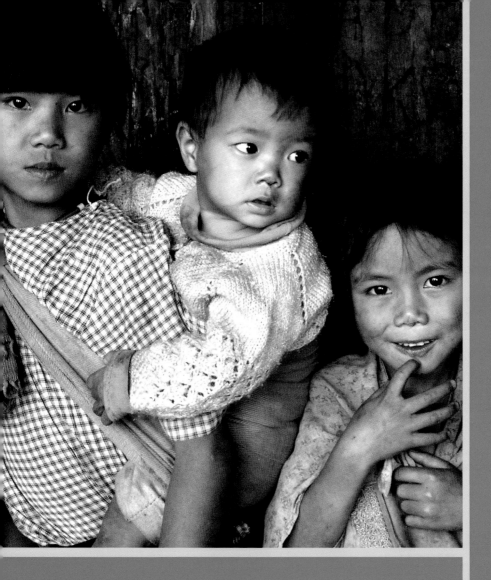

1

**International Financial Institutions:
Policy Review and Impacts on Indigenous
Peoples in Asia**

Rhoda Dalang
Jill Cariño

I. Introduction

The United Nations Development Programme (UNDP) is the United Nation's global development network, advocating for change and connecting countries to knowledge, experience and resources to help people build better lives.

The UNDP corporate mandate, development cooperation processes and agreements, and the aspirations of indigenous peoples guide UNDP engagement with indigenous peoples and their organizations. In the context of the International Decade of the World's Indigenous People (1995-2004), and building on previous initiatives, UNDP issued a policy guidance note in August 2001 entitled: *UNDP and Indigenous Peoples: A Policy of Engagement.*

In the Asia-Pacific region, in recognition of the large number of indigenous peoples in the region and UNDP's mandate to promote democratic governance, UNDP initiated a new programme for indigenous peoples – the Regional Initiative on Indigenous Peoples' Rights and Development (RIPP). The aim of the regional programme is to provide a space at the regional level for dialogue and cooperation amongst and between the national governments, donors, development agencies and indigenous peoples in the region. RIPP works in close cooperation with its partners to ensure a participatory and rights-based approach to development.

Many of international financial institutions (IFIs) – key actors in development initiatives in the region – have policies and guidelines to guide their work with indigenous peoples. In response to a request from indigenous peoples – a direct reflection of UNDP's position of trust and neutrality – RIPP is engaged in establishing a process of dialogue between IFIs, key development financing agencies and indigenous peoples through advocacy and training.

The most relevant IFIs in Asia are the Asian Development Bank (ADB), the Japan Bank for International Cooperation (JBIC) and the World Bank (WB). Projects developed and implemented by these institutions have significant impacts on the rights and livelihoods of indigenous peoples throughout the region. In recognition of this, WB and ADB have developed indigenous peoples' policies to guide project development and funding – or are in the process of reviewing and/or adopting new ones. Indigenous peoples have voiced significant concerns regarding these policies and their implementation. In response, some of these institutions have indicated their willingness to engage with indigenous peoples in the review and consultation regarding these policies. There is thus an opportunity to initiate a process of dialogue and engagement between indigenous peoples and IFIs in order to develop more responsive adaptation and implementation of indigenous-related programmes through the policy framework.

However, there is a lack of awareness among many indigenous peoples regarding the policies of IFIs. For them to engage in an effective and constructive manner in the policy dialogue with the major financial institutions, there is an urgent need for indigenous peoples to be better informed on the role, mandate, policies and programs of the IFIs. Concurrently, it is also imperative to provide a space for dialogue between indigenous peoples and international financial institutions to ensure indigenous peoples' voices are heard and heeded, especially during policy review processes.

The general framework used in the analysis is based largely on the principles and approaches enshrined in the Human Rights-Based Approach to Development and international instruments and jurisprudence which are minimum standards in evaluating the policies and practices as they relate with indigenous peoples. The international instruments most relevant to indigenous peoples include the following:

- Universal Declaration of Human Rights, 1948

- Convention on the Prevention and Punishment of the Crime of Genocide, 1951

- International Labour Organization Convention No. 107 on Indigenous and Tribal Populations, 1957

- The International Covenant on Civil and Political Rights, 1966

- The International Covenant on Economic, Social and Cultural Rights, 1966

- The International Convention on the Elimination of All Forms of Racial Discrimination (ICERD), 1966 and Recommendation XXIII (51) of the ICERD Committee on the Rights of Indigenous Peoples (18 August 1997)

- Convention on the Elimination of Discrimination Against Women, 1979

- International Labour Organization Convention No. 169 on Indigenous and Tribal Peoples, 1989

- Convention on the Rights of the Child, 1990

- Rio Declaration on Environment and Development and Agenda 21, 1992

- Convention on Biological Diversity, 1992

- Framework Convention on Climate Change, 1992

- Convention to Combat Desertification, 1994

- African Charter of Human and Peoples' Rights, 1981

- European Council Resolution on Indigenous Peoples within the Framework of the Development Cooperation of the Community and Member States, 1998

- Durban Declaration and Program of Action, 2001

- Vienna Declaration and Programme Action, 1993

- United Nations Declaration on the Rights of Indigenous Peoples (draft)

- Organization of American States Declaration on the Rights of Indigenous Peoples, 1997 (draft)

The paper is a consolidated digest of three case studies pertaining to the World Bank Group (WBG), prepared by Fergus Mackay; ADB, prepared by Devasish Roy; and the JBIC, prepared by Joan Carling and Friends of the Earth Japan. It is an effort to contribute towards informing the various development stakeholders on the policies and practices of these international financial institutions related to indigenous peoples.

II. Background of major international financial institutions

World Bank Group

The World Bank (WB) was founded in 1944, along with its sister organization the International Monetary Fund (IMF), following the United Nations Monetary and Financial Conference hosted by the US Treasury Department at Bretton Woods, USA. Thus they are also known as the Bretton Woods Institutions.[1]

The WB was established as an intergovernmental organization with the primary mandate of financing reconstruction and facilitating economic development post World War II.[2] After the war, the industrialized countries wanted to ensure that the capitalist economy would be strengthened and expanded worldwide. International institutions that could guarantee this had to be set up, thus the creation of the WB and IMF. The WB's role was to promote the international flow of capital to help rebuild the once-rich countries destroyed in World War II.[3]

The World Bank Group (WBG) is actually a group of five specialized institutions:

- The International Bank for Reconstruction and Development (IBRD) makes development loans, guarantees loans and offers analytical and advisory services;

- The International Development Association (IDA) gives loans to countries that are deemed 'usually not creditworthy' in financial markets;

- The International Finance Corporation (IFC) is the largest multilateral source of loan and equity financing for private sector projects in the developing world;

- The Multilateral Investment Guarantee Agency (MIGA) provides investment guarantees;

- The International Center for Settlement of Investment Disputes (ICSID) facilitates the settlement of investment disputes between governments and foreign investors.

The IBRD and the IDA are considered to be the public sector arms of the WBG, while the IFC and the MIGA are WBG's private sector arms.[4]

---

[1] Ibon Foundation. "International Financial Institutions and Indigenous Peoples in the Philippines." Paper presented during the Taking Control of our Resources Workshop on Indigenous Peoples, International Financial Institutions and Multinational Companies organized by Cordillera Peoples' Alliance, 17-19 Dec. 2004, Quezon City, Philippines.

[2] Fergus MacKay. "Indigenous Peoples and the Asian Development Framework: Multilateral Development Banks and Development Agreements. Indigenous Peoples and the World Bank Group." Case Study Paper prepared for the workshop on Indigenous Peoples and Rights-Based Development: Engaging in Dialogue sponsored by UNDP-RIPP, November 4-6, 2005, Baguio City, Philippines. A final version of this paper is also included in this publication.

[3] Victoria Tauli-Corpuz. "The World Bank, the International Monetary Fund, and the Erosion of Indigenous Economic Systems." *Indigenous Perspectives* Vol. 3, No. 1: 10-37 (June 2000).

[4] Ibon Foundation, "International Financial Institutions."

Unlike the United Nations which practices a one-country one-vote system, the WB has a one-dollar one vote system where voting power is determined by the amount of financial contributions of member countries. The Group of Seven – United States, United Kingdom, Canada, Japan, Germany, France and Italy – hold 40 to 45 percent of the votes by virtue of their contributions; the United States alone holds 16.5 percent of the voting power. It has also become a tradition to have an American as the WB president. The WBG's mandate and stated objective is "to help reduce poverty and finance investments that contribute to economic growth." Its main activities are to provide loans or guarantee credit for projects such as roads, bridges, power plants, transport, schools, and other infrastructure that will support the operations of governments and private corporations. Its primary lending instruments are:

- Project investment loans to fund dams, irrigation projects, schools, hospitals, mining, etc.;

- Structural adjustment loans and sectoral adjustment loans;

- Hybrid loans which combine elements of adjustment and project investment components. This can include funding for policy or legal reforms like changing Mining Acts, Forestry Laws, etc.[5]

The WBG is one of the largest financers of development projects and activities in the world. In 1999-2000, the Bank's cumulative lending alone was US$162,789 million.[6] The Bank has also played a fundamental role in the globalization of extractive industries (EI), both by financing specific projects and by providing investment and insurance guarantees, and, more importantly, through structural and sectoral adjustment loans and technical assistance projects designed to revise legislation and reform government institutions.[7]

Asian Development Bank

The Asian Development Bank (ADB) is an international financial institution that was established on 19 December 1966. It has 61 member countries, consisting of 44 regional and 17 non-regional members. Its mission is to help its developing country members (DCMs) reduce poverty and improve their living conditions through its "strategic agenda" of sustainable economic growth, inclusive social development and governance with effective policies. It has three cross-cutting themes:

- Private sector development,

- Regional cooperation and integration for development, and

- Environmental sustainability.[8]

5 Tauli-Corpuz. "Erosion of Indigenous Economic Systems." pp. 12-14.

6 Fergus MacKay, "Making Molehills out of Mountains: Indigenous Peoples, the World Bank and Extractive Industries Review." 2005.

7 MacKay, "Indigenous Peoples and the World Bank Group."

8 Ibon Foundation, "International Financial Institutions."

The ADB's principal functions are to grant loans and equity investments for its DCMs and to provide technical assistance in development projects. It likewise promotes investments of public and private capital and provides assistance in coordinating development policies. Its operations cover agriculture and agro-industry, energy, industry and non-fuel minerals, finance, transport and communications, social infrastructure and other sectors. The highest policy-making body in the ADB is the Board of Governors, which meets annually. It is composed of representatives of each member country. However, its operations are delegated to its 12-member Board of Directors and the Bank President. The Board of Directors has the sole authority to decide on the Bank's loans, guarantees, borrowings, technical assistance, equity investments and other activities. The Bank President handles the day-to-day operations.[9]

Although developing countries dominate the membership of the ADB, the real power rests in the member-countries who have the highest capital stock or shareholding, which determines their voting power. Traditionally these large shareholders have been members of the Organization of Economic Cooperation and Development (OECD), a group of 21 First World donor countries including Japan, US, Germany, France and the United Kingdom. Of these countries, Japan and the US have the highest combined shareholdings of almost 32 percent of total subscribed capital, and thus, account for 13 percent each of the total voting power.

The combined voting power of the OECD countries has resulted in a shift of ADB's loan operations. In the first 20 years of its existence, the ADB emphasized project financing – mainly loans to agriculture and large-scale infrastructure projects, such as roads and hydropower dams – and the encouragement of export-oriented industries and a strong regulatory role for the state. However, in the wake of the founding of the World Trade Organization (WTO), with the push for greater liberalization of developing countries, the ADB stressed the central importance of private sector development and foreign capital, with a reduced role for the state and lending for structural adjustment and policy objectives as opposed to individual projects.[10]

Japan Bank for International Cooperation

The Japan Bank for International Cooperation (JBIC) is the second largest development bank in the world. It was established in 1999 when two large Japanese financial institutions, namely the Japan Export-Import Bank (JEXIM) and the Overseas Economic Cooperation Fund (OECF), merged.[11]

---

[9] Ibid.

[10] Ibid.

[11] Joan Carling and Friends of the Earth-Japan. "Japan Bank for International Cooperation Guidelines for Confirmation of Environmental and Social Considerations: Its implications to Indigenous Peoples". Case Study Paper prepared for the workshop on Indigenous Peoples and Rights Based Development: Engaging in Dialogue sponsored by UNDP-RIPP, 4-6 November 2005, Baguio City, Philippines. A final version of this paper is also included as Chapter 3 in this publication.

OECF was mainly responsible for providing Yen Loans, one type of official development assistance (ODA). According to the Japanese Government, the purpose of Yen Loans is to promote the economic development and welfare of developing countries. JEXIM did other kinds of international financial operations (IFOs) that were not ODA loans, such as export loans, import loans, investment loans, and untied loans. The purpose of IFOs is to support Japanese companies' exports and investments.[12]

JBIC, as it combined these two institutions together, is responsible for both Yen Loans as well as the IFOs. Therefore, JBIC lends to governments of developing countries, and to Japanese and foreign companies. Currently, it finances projects all around the world, but most of the projects JBIC finances are in Asia (approximately 80 percent in 2002).[13] Much of Japanese ODA is used to fund infrastructure projects such as highways, power generation projects, water facilities, airports, flood control projects and construction of ports. The majority is in the form of loans, rather than grants, leading to increased indebtedness of borrowing countries.

Another important issue is the nature of ODA as 'tied aid' or aid given on the condition that it can be spent only on goods and services from the donor country. Although aid from Japan is today generally 'untied', allowing associated goods and services to be acquired from any country, there are pressures from the Japanese business community to re-tie ODA in order to create profit-generating opportunities for Japanese corporations. A 2003 revision to the ODA Charter puts explicit stress on Japan's national interest, with the objective "to contribute to the peace and development of the international community, and thereby to help ensure Japan's own security and prosperity", as opposed to the more 'humanitarian viewpoint' in the previous Charter.[14]

III. Experiences of indigenous peoples in Asia with IFI-funded projects

The indigenous peoples in Asia have had much experience with projects funded by IFIs. The following are some concrete examples to illustrate the key aspects of this relationship:

Support for extractive industries

The WBG's support for oil, gas and mining projects is facilitating exploitation of developing countries' natural resources by transnational corporations, at the expense of indigenous peoples and affected local communities. Increasing foreign investments in natural resource exploitation often yield profits for multinational corporations and the local elite that rarely trickle down to indigenous peoples and frequently exacerbate poverty and compromise cultural integrity and security.[15]

---

[12] Ibid.

[13] Ibid.

[14] Ibon Foundation, "International Financial Institutions."

[15] MacKay, "Making Molehills out of Mountains."

1

One example is the IFC's support for the Climax Arimco Mining Company's (CAMC) proposed community development plan in Didipio, Philippines. The IFC consultant claimed that the acceptance by the host community of the development plan represented the 'best case' of prior informed consent he had ever witnessed. The CAMC set up the Didipio Gold/Copper Project after being granted a Financial and Technical Assistance Agreement (FTAA) by the Philippine Government in 1994 covering 37,000 hectares for mining exploration and development activities. The community protested the mining activities, and soldiers were assigned to the area to secure CAMC operations. There were also reports of harassment and other abuses committed by the soldiers and para-military forces.[16]

A JBIC-funded extractive industry project is the Sakhalin II Oil Development Project in Russia to develop oil and natural gas reserves for export to Japan, Korea and other countries, which will cause serious damage to the indigenous peoples of the North Sakhalin Region as well as to the fisheries and ecosystems in the Sea of Okhotsk.[17]

Participation of indigenous peoples in decision-making

A potentially positive example of ADB involvement in indigenous peoples' area is the Chittagong Hill Tracts (CHT) Rural Development Project in Bangladesh. The project was initiated with the support of the indigenous peoples in the CHT region, particularly the Chittagong Hill Tracts Regional Council, an apex body formed as a result of a peace accord agreed in 1997. The indigenous chairperson of the Regional Council is the *ex-officio* chairperson of the project's Regional Coordination Committee, with three indigenous district council chairpersons and three traditional paramount chiefs as members.[18]

The project's primary focus is to reduce 'absolute poverty in the Chittagong Hill Tracts and to provide a confidence-building environment for the Peace Accord of 1997.' The project also includes a Community Development component with a programme on Legal Literacy, Training and Gender. The loan agreement between the ADB and the Government of Bangladesh refers to the monitoring and implementation of an Indigenous Peoples Development Plan by the project-monitoring unit. The involvement of indigenous peoples' institutions in decision-making and project implementation is a desirable development. However, the potentially positive impact of the project is at risk because of certain features that have been included without the knowledge and consent of the people concerned, in particular, the inclusion of a micro-credit component.[19]

Another illustration is the WB-funded Conservation of Priority Protected Areas Project (CPPAP 1994-2001), a seven-year, $20-million grant to conserve the Philippines' mega-diversity of flora and fauna – under the WB's Global Environment Facility. The project's goals are to provide support for conservation, management and development of protected areas and to involve local indigenous communities in the management of protected areas through their representation in Protected Area Management Boards.

---

[16] Ibon Foundation, "International Financial Institutions."

[17] Carling and Friends of the Earth-Japan. "JBIC Guidelines: Implications to Indigenous Peoples."

[18] Raja Devasish Roy. "The Asian Development Bank's Indigenous Peoples' Policy and its Impact upon Indigenous Peoples of Asia." Case Study Paper prepared for the workshop on Indigenous Peoples and Rights Based Development: Engaging in Dialogue, sponsored by UNDP-RIPP, 4-6 November 2005, Baguio City, Philippines. A final version of this paper is also included as Chapter 2 in this publication.

[19] Ibid.

Studies indicated that the affected indigenous peoples were not involved in the planning of the CPPAP. The project was conceptualized 'for' indigenous peoples and not 'with' them. However, there was some space for the affected indigenous communities to express their concerns through their representation in the Protected Areas Management Boards. The communities also complained that the project restricted their traditional use of forest resources, which are important for their survival. Another concern was the delay in the release of funds for the livelihood component of the project.[20]

Inappropriate projects

The lack of consultation, participation in decision-making, and free, prior-informed consent of indigenous peoples in development projects affecting them often lead to inappropriate, unwanted or unnecessary projects.

A case in point is the JBIC-funded Kelau Dam, which aims to provide water to Selangor State and Kuala Lumpur in Malaysia by transferring around 1.5 billion litres of water per day from the Kelau River in Pahang State to the Langat River in Selangor State. The dam will have serious impacts on the Kelau River ecosystem and will require the resettlement of 325 Orang Asli (indigenous people) and 120 Malay farmers, with serious repercussions on their lives and livelihoods. Studies by Malaysian non-government organizations (NGOs) show that the current water supply system in Selangor State is wasteful and beset with inefficiencies. Investment in water conservation measures and reduction in system losses could result in water savings that would make the construction of the Kelau Dam unnecessary. Although the project proponents claim that the people are agreeable to the project, the Centre for Orang Asli Concerns (COAC) found that the affected Temuan families did not give their free, prior and informed consent to the relocation.[21]

Another example is the ADB-funded Community Forestry Program in the Chittagong Hill Tracts in Bangladesh implemented during the 1980s. The programme called *'joutha khamar'* or 'collective farming' was intended to end shifting cultivation by the Jummas by forcibly relocating them to settled farms. The project resulted in the forced evacuation and dispossession of the indigenous Jumma peoples of their land in favour of Bengali settlers. It also allowed unhindered and accelerated exploitation of the forest and its resources, pushed the Jumma people into a state of constant debt and created dependence of Jumma people on the Bengali moneylenders and traders.[22]

Privatization and transnational corporations

The privatization of industries, services and natural resources by transnational corporations is based on the rationale that most state corporations are inefficiently run mainly as a result of corruption. Therefore, if these are transferred to the private sector, they can be run more

---

[20] Ibon Foundation, "International Financial Institutions."

[21] Carling and Friends of the Earth-Japan. "JBIC Guidelines: Implications to Indigenous Peoples."

[22] Suhas Chakma. "ADB Programs in Bangladesh: Identifying Critical Issues." *Indigenous Perspectives* Vol. 3, No. 1: 140-150 (June 2000).

efficiently resulting in better products and services. However, privatization schemes under structural adjustment programmes of the World Bank have brought tragic results for the indigenous peoples and the environment.[23]

A case in Orissa, a northeast state of India, as cited by Corpuz, makes this clear. As part of the scheme to transfer energy-intensive industries to the south, fossil fuel-powered plants were needed. Privatization of the energy sector was seen as the best option, and, therefore, the power sector was privatized through the structural adjustment programme of the World Bank. The coal-powered plants, which the state operated, were sold to the private sector. WB provided only 3 percent of the needed investment, the private sector and ODA provided the rest. As a result, various transnational corporations from the United States, France, Canada and Japan earned $290 billion in combined total sales from procurement contracts in Orissa's power sector. The State of Orissa got $2.85 billion in various loans and financial assistance. Meanwhile, the indigenous peoples, who make up 25 percent of Orissa's population, along with people from other marginalized sectors such as the farmers and fishers, got the worst deal. After this energy-intensive, toxic, industrial development, their lives worsened: their subsistence economies were destroyed, health problems increased, communities were displaced, power costs increased beyond the reach of the majority population and human rights violations were committed against workers and tribal populations.[24]

Impact on culture and standards of living

Some of the development projects funded by IFIs are insensitive to local indigenous cultures and have caused a decline in their living standards.

The Koto Panjang Dam in West Sumatra, Indonesia, built with loans from JBIC in the 1990s, relocated some 4,886 households of the Minagkabau ethnic group. The project's feasibility study failed to take into account the characteristics of Minagkabau society. The villagers were resettled in a place that had no communal land (*ulayat*) or building (*rumah gadang*). Housing provided by the government was not the traditional style on stilts, but wooden houses poorly built directly on the ground. Some of the new mosques were built facing the wrong direction and others were too small, so the people had to then build their own mosques. In addition, existing relationships in Minagkabau society were ruined when people lost respect for village leaders who accepted bribes and had difficulty coping with resettlement. The people's traditional lifestyle and culture were destroyed and their living standards declined considerably.[25]

Another case is an ADB-funded agricultural programme in the Cordillera region of the Philippines. The Cordillera Highland Agricultural Resource Management (CHARM) Project, which started in 1996, promoted agriculture for the market and encouraged communities to supplant traditional subsistence production in favour of cash crops such as high-yield rice, cut-flowers and commercial vegetables and fruits. This resulted in the extinction of

---

[23] Tauli-Corpuz, "Erosion of Indigenous Economic Systems." p. 25.

[24] Ibid. pp. 26-27.

[25] Carling and Friends of the Earth-Japan. "JBIC Guidelines: Implications to Indigenous Peoples."

indigenous varieties of crops and has made indigenous farmers increasingly dependent on buying expensive agricultural techno-packs of seeds, chemical pesticides and fertilizers leading to perpetual indebtedness.[26]

Displacement

There are a number of examples of the displacement of indigenous populations. The following is illustrative of the impacts this has on the traditional livelihoods.

The San Roque Multi-purpose Project, funded by JBIC, displaced more than 4,400 people in the Philippines, and threatens the livelihood of thousands of indigenous Ibaloi people living along the Agno River upstream of the dam. Approximately 20,000 residents of Itogon, Benguet, will be affected by the sediment that is expected to accumulate behind the reservoir over the course of the dam's life. This sediment will eventually submerge homes, rice terraces, orchards, pasturelands, gardens and burial grounds of the Ibaloi living close to the Agno River. The fertile lands along the river and the gold ore found in the mountains have sustained Ibaloi communities engaged in agriculture, fishing and small-scale gold panning for generations. Project proponents did not obtain the free and prior informed consent of affected indigenous communities. Consultations were conducted only after the project was already underway. The energy project was completed and commercial operation began in March 2003.[27]

Another case is the proposed Laiban dam project in Quezon Province, Philippines, which is part of an ADB-funded programme to develop new water sources for Metro Manila. The project will direct 2,400 million litres of water daily to Metro Manila. A $3.26 million technical assistance loan was given by the ADB to the Metropolitan Waterworks and Sewerage System to implement the project together with private concessionaires Manila Water and Maynilad Water Services. The dam will directly affect around 20,000 hectares of land, deplete the irrigation supply of lowland farmers in Quezon province, and displace some 10,000 indigenous peoples, and upland settlers. Negotiations for resettlement are ongoing, with the indigenous Dumagat people reluctant to leave their ancestral territory as they fear this will result in the loss of their traditional culture. There are also reports of increasing militarization in the affected areas and recruitment of paramilitary CAFGU members among the Dumagat and Remontado tribes.[28]

IV. Lessons learned and recommendations for strategic engagement

From the above-mentioned examples, some key lessons and recommendations can be drawn that can help improve the implementation of development projects and the relations between IFIs and affected indigenous peoples.

---

[26] Ibon Foundation, "International Financial Institutions."

[27] Carling and Friends of the Earth Japan. "JBIC Guidelines: Implications to Indigenous Peoples."

[28] Ibon Foundation, "International Financial Institutions."

Need to properly assess social and environmental impacts prior to approval

There is a need to adequately assess the all projects social and environmental impacts, with the participation of the peoples concerned, prior to project approval. While WB, in principle, does undertake environmental and social impact assessments (ESIA) prior to project approval, the more relevant issue is to ensure indigenous peoples' participation in and free prior and informed consent to ESIAs. Failure to do so could result in impacts far beyond what was originally predicted.

Need to provide adequate information to ensure free, prior and informed consent of indigenous peoples

IFIs and project developers need to provide adequate information to communities that may be affected by a project and to the public, especially critical documents such as a clear explanation of what the project is, and the following environmental impact assessments and resettlement plans.

Adequate monitoring and evaluation during and after project implementation

Better monitoring and evaluation procedures need to be established, with the IFIs taking more responsibility for implementing, monitoring and evaluating projects, instead of leaving these activities entirely in the hands of government or private sector partners. Affected communities should be provided with access and recourse to the IFIs as project funders, especially in those situations where compensation payments are not honoured. The IFIs have the ultimate responsibility to ensure that the projects are undertaken in accordance with their own policies and international human rights standards.

Need to establish mechanisms to deal with outstanding problems

Many projects have resulted in communities being worse off than they were before. Yet no mechanism is available for dealing with the serious environmental and social problems that may be created by projects. There is a growing demand for IFIs to take responsibility for repairing damage caused by its previously funded projects by allocating resources for retroactive compensation, mitigation and rehabilitation measures.

Based on the case papers on WB, ADB and JBIC, the following are recommendations for strategic engagement with these IFI's:

Participatory process of policy review and reform

The modalities for a future process of review of the WB and ADB's Indigenous Peoples policies should include indigenous peoples and incorporate their recommendations and suggestions for improvement. Such consultations may need to be preceded by an in-depth evaluation of the diverse impacts upon indigenous peoples of IFI-funded projects, which can feed into a future revision process.

Regarding the review process of the WB's OP 4.10, Mackay suggests establishing national and regional working groups to systematically identify and track WB projects applying OP

4.10, with the aim of providing well-documented inputs to the three-year review of the OP agreed to by the Board. These groups could advocate, together with indigenous peoples from other regions, for full indigenous participation in the three-year review of the WB policy.

It is also recommended that WB cooperate with or establish mechanisms to guarantee the full and effective participation of indigenous peoples in defining the meaning and application of free, prior and informed consultation and ascertaining broad community support. One such mechanism is the UN Permanent Forum on Indigenous Issues, in which WB itself participates through the Inter-Agency Support Group. Furthermore, it is important for indigenous peoples to proactively seek to define free, prior and informed consultation and broad community support in ways that are consistent with indigenous peoples' traditional or accepted methods of collective decision-making.

Likewise, the policy formulation of JBIC on indigenous peoples must ensure the direct engagement of indigenous peoples and their participation in the process in order to ensure that their views, concerns and issues are taken into account and integrated in the finalization of the policy.

Dissemination of information

Dissemination of data and information, in a manner and form understandable by indigenous peoples, is crucial to ensuring transparency and accountability on the part of the IFIs. For WB, it is necessary that concerned indigenous organizations, peoples and communities affected by WB projects are well-informed about the requirements of OP 4.10 and other related OPs and can thus advocate for greater conformity with WB's own policies on indigenous peoples.

Environmental and social impact studies to consider particular impacts on indigenous peoples

Environmental and social impact studies should take full account of the specificities of indigenous peoples, and include socio-cultural impacts, intergenerational livelihood activities, and the views of affected indigenous peoples on compensation or non-compensation of losses, which are beyond material measures. These studies should ensure a process of transparency and validation of affected communities, prior to consideration for project funding.

Monitoring evaluation of project impact on indigenous peoples

The experience of the European Commission (EC) in having some of its projects evaluated by indigenous experts, and the findings shared among indigenous peoples and EC project staff and policy-level officials, can provide ideas for similar evaluation exercises for WB, ADB and JBIC-funded projects in indigenous peoples' areas in future.

Indigenous peoples have demanded that WB involve local, national and regional indigenous organizations in actively tracking and monitoring WB operations throughout the whole project cycle. Such needs are equally relevant in the case of ADB and JBIC.

Influencing policy reforms and decision-making by member country Governments

The implementation of the ADB's Policy on Indigenous Peoples is affected by relevant policies of the borrower governments. Thus, the positive impact of the ADB's policy could be watered down or countered in the absence of adequate national laws and policies recognizing indigenous peoples' rights.

It is recommended that the ADB engage the concerned national governments to initiate policy reforms in their countries in order to effectively implement the ADB's policy on Indigenous Peoples. It is important in this respect to encourage ADB member governments to consult indigenous peoples in their countries, using participatory methods of consultation.

In principle, WB-funded projects have to respect national laws. In cases when national laws contain higher levels of protection for indigenous peoples' rights than WB Operational Policy (OP) 4.10, as in the case of the Philippines' Indigenous Peoples' Rights Act, it is necessary to assess projects in relation to higher national legal standards in addition to OP 4.10.

It is also important to identify those in government with primary responsibility for IFI projects and policy in order to understand their thinking. In some cases, this may be helped by also involving national agencies responsible for indigenous issues, legislative committees and other concerned bodies in the dialogue. It could also be useful to develop working relations with the Indigenous Peoples' Unit in the ADB.

Including indigenous peoples in bank-member country negotiations

The ADB policy clearly declares that 'the fundamental relationship between ADB and governments remains the basis for country-specific operations'. Indigenous peoples, however, are unaware of the contractual relationship between the bank and borrower governments. This needs to be corrected by indigenous participation both in the deliberations of ADB, and in policy dialogues with concerned governments.

From as early as possible in the project cycle, it is necessary to identify, inform and advise affected indigenous communities and monitor ADB-financed projects. Identifying projects early in the cycle is critical in influencing project design and subsequent implementation.

Consultants are usually employed by IFIs in the design of projects. It is therefore important to identify and communicate with consultants, particularly those addressing indigenous peoples' issues and legal issues. It is also important to identify the whole range of financiers in any IFI-funded project and to communicate indigenous peoples' concerns to all donors involved. It is not uncommon for certain donors to take on more supportive positions in relation to indigenous peoples' rights than WB.

Accountability measures and litigation for violations of own policies and guidelines

It is recommended to institute accountability measures on the part of IFIs in relation to violations of their own policies and guidelines. These should include measures on compensation of affected communities, mitigation and rehabilitation of damaged environment and providing resources for people's livelihood. Another avenue is the Inspection Panel of the World Bank but this is limited to non-compliance of WB with its internal policies and procedures.[29]

V. Conclusions

A review of the policies, programmes, projects and impacts of IFI-funded development on indigenous peoples in Asia underscores the need to ensure that the benefits of development do not just 'trickle down' to the poor and marginalized sectors, including indigenous peoples, but rather fully address their needs and improve their conditions.

At this point, there is a need for indigenous peoples to actively participate in policy review, reform and advocacy in relation to development programmes that may be planned for implementation within their communities. Indigenous peoples' engagement with IFIs and other development actors is necessary in order to ensure that indigenous peoples' rights are respected and promoted in any development endeavour.

Advocacy efforts of indigenous peoples could be directed at achieving reforms of existing policies of IFI through a participatory process of review and consultation. These reforms could also cover national policies of member country governments so that these are consistent with IFI policies and international human rights standards on indigenous peoples. Including indigenous peoples' perspectives in loan negotiations between IFIs and borrower countries is also another way forward.

Another area for advocacy is to push for the conduct of environmental assessment and social impact studies that consider particular impacts on indigenous peoples. It is also necessary to work for more effective monitoring and evaluation of development project's impact on indigenous peoples, such as soliciting case studies and reviews by indigenous experts, and to put into place measures that will hold IFIs accountable for violations of their own policies and guidelines.

In engaging with IFIs, it is crucial to challenge their policies and practices pertaining to indigenous peoples by weighing these against international standards as the minimum. It is also necessary to assert the indigenous peoples' inherent right to land, territories, resources and self-determination as the fundamental yardstick. It is only in the context of fundamental reforms and a shift towards a rights-based approach that development aid can truly be said to contribute to the genuine development of indigenous peoples.

---

[29] See MacKay, "Indigenous Peoples and the World Bank Group" for more details.

Sources

Carling, Joan and Friends of the Earth-Japan. "Japan Bank for International Cooperation (JBIC) Guidelines for Confirmation of Environmental and Social Considerations: Its implications to Indigenous Peoples." Case Study Paper presented during the workshop on Indigenous Peoples and Rights-Based Development: Engaging in Dialogue, sponsored by UNDP-RIPP, 4-6 November 2005, Baguio City, Philippines.

Chakma, Suhas. "ADB Programs in Bangladesh: Identifying Critical Issues." *Indigenous Perspectives* Vol. 3, No. 1, June 2000. pp. 140-150.

Griffiths, Tom. "Indigenous Peoples and the World Bank: Experiences with Participation." July 2005.

Ibon Foundation. "International Financial Institutions and Indigenous Peoples in the Philippines." Paper presented during the Taking Control of our Resources Workshop on Indigenous Peoples, International Financial Institutions and Multinational Companies, organized by Cordillera Peoples' Alliance, 17-19 Dec. 2004, Quezon City, Philippines.

Kingsbury, Benedict. Operational Policies of International Institutions as Part of Law Making Process: The World Bank and Indigenous Peoples. 1999.

MacKay, Fergus. "Making Molehills out of Mountains: Indigenous Peoples, the World Bank and Extractive Industries Review." 2005.

_____. "Indigenous Peoples and the Asian Development Framework: Multilateral Development Banks and Development Agreements. Indigenous Peoples and the World Bank Group." Case Study Paper prepared for the workshop on Indigenous Peoples and Rights Based Development: Engaging in Dialogue, sponsored by UNDP-RIPP, 4-6 November 2005, Baguio City, Philippines.

Roy, Raja Devasish. "The Asian Development Bank's Indigenous Peoples' Policy and its Impact upon Indigenous Peoples of Asia". Case Study Paper presented during the workshop on Indigenous Peoples and Rights Based Development: Engaging in Dialogue, sponsored by UNDP-RIPP, 4-6 November 2005, Baguio City, Philippines.

Tauli-Corpuz, Victoria. "The World Bank, the International Monetary Fund, and the Erosion of Indigenous Economic Systems." *Indigenous Perspectives*, Vol. 3, No. 1. June 2000. pp. 10-35.

2

The Asian Development Bank and
Indigenous Peoples in Asia

Raja Devasish Roy

I. Scope of the policy

The Asian Development Bank (ADB)'s Policy on Indigenous Peoples is triggered when negative impacts of an ADB-supported project are anticipated.[1] In such a situation, "adequate measures must be taken to mitigate the negative impact, or make certain that a compensation plan ensuring that project-affected people are as well off with the project as without it".[2] The policy applies to both public and private sector operations.[3] It defines or identifies indigenous peoples in a broad manner and includes one or more of the following:

- Descent from pre-state population groups;

- Maintenance of cultural and other identities, institutions, etc. that are distinct from mainstream society;

- Self-identification, identification by others and desire to maintain its cultural identity;

- Distinct linguistic identity;

- Orientation towards traditional economic systems; and

- Attachment to traditional habitats and territories.[4]

In addition, a working definition is employed as an operational tool, which reads:

> "Indigenous peoples should be regarded as those with a social or cultural identity distinct from the dominant or mainstream society, which makes them vulnerable to being disadvantaged in the process of development."[5]

The ambit or scope of the application of the ADB's Policy on Indigenous Peoples is clarified in the document itself, which states:

> "The policy, together with practices addressing indigenous peoples, **applies in parallel with and does not replace or supersede other ADB policies and practices**. Each of the **elements of the policy** and practice addressing indigenous peoples **are considered within the context of national development policies and approaches**, and the fundamental relationship between ADB and governments remains the basis for country-specific operations (emphasis added)."[6]

To rephrase the above, the policy itself advises us that in order to understand the full implications of ADB-funded projects upon indigenous peoples, we must look, in addition to the specific policy itself, into the following:

---

[1] Asian Development Bank, *Policy on Indigenous Peoples*, pp. 2, 9.

[2] Ibid.

[3] Ibid. p. 17.

[4] Ibid. p. 6.

[5] Ibid. Case-specific identification may also be addressed at the stage of *Initial Social Assessment*. See also, pp. 6, 7 and Appendix.

[6] Ibid. p. 25. The same paragraph further provides the following (at p. 25): "The strategies and approaches employed by ADB in relation to indigenous peoples build on the existing strategic framework and operational experience. The policy addressing indigenous peoples complements and supports, and is complemented and supported by other ADB policies. Compliance with the policy on indigenous peoples does not obviate the requirement of compliance with other ADB policies."

Indigenous Peoples and the Human Rights-Based Approach to Development

(a) Other relevant ADB policies;

(b) Relevant ADB practices;

(c) Development policies and approaches of the borrower government; and

(d) Nature of the relationship between the ADB and the concerned borrower government.

Therefore, it appears that although the ADB's Policy on Indigenous Peoples applies equally to all its member countries, the nature of its actual impact on the ground would *vary from country to country*. It would depend upon such factors as the ADB's numerous policies and practices in addition to its Policy on Indigenous Peoples; the relevant policies and practices of the borrower governments; and the dynamics of the ADB-borrower relationship. Case studies of field-level experiences related to ADB-funded projects in areas inhabited by indigenous peoples would provide added insights into the matter under study.

II. Basic elements of the policy

One of the salient elements of the ADB's Policy on Indigenous Peoples is to "avoid negatively impacting indigenous peoples" through ADB operations. Where that is not possible, the policy is to provide "adequate and appropriate compensation".[7] When substantial negative impacts on indigenous peoples are anticipated, the first step is to conduct an *initial social assessment* or ISA, which is mandatory for all ADB projects.[8] The policy recommends that an ISA be initiated in the early stages of a project.[9] The ISA addresses the key social dimensions of the project, as well as the needs, demands and capacities of the people concerned.[10] It also identifies the project beneficiaries and the people that are likely to be adversely affected by the concerned project.[11]

If the ISA determines that indigenous peoples are likely to be adversely impacted, or that indigenous peoples suffer from disadvantage or are otherwise vulnerable in the project intervention process, an Indigenous Peoples' Development Plan must be prepared by the borrower government or other project sponsor to address the relevant needs or disadvantages, as the case may be.[12] Where appropriate, the Indigenous Peoples' Development Plan is expected to be used to redesign a project in order to decrease or mitigate negative impacts, or to provide adequate compensation, in addition to mitigating harm or damage.[13] The policy recognizes that consultation with indigenous peoples' groups

---

[7] Ibid.

[8] Ibid. p. 18. See further, (i) *Guidelines for Incorporation of Social Dimensions in Bank Operations*, Asian Development Bank, Manila, October 1993; (ii) *Handbook for Incorporation of Social Dimensions in Projects*, Asian Development Bank, Manila, May 1994.

[9] Ibid. p. 18.

[10] Ibid.

[11] Ibid. pp. 18, 19.

[12] Ibid. pp. 19, 20.

[13] Ibid. p. 19.

is "key to developing an effective, accurate, and responsive indigenous peoples development plan". Consequently, it appears to consider consultation with affected peoples as mandatory.[14] The elaborate provisions on the Indigenous Peoples Development Plan include suggestions to consider the wishes of the affected indigenous peoples and their social and cultural patterns; capacity building of the concerned communities, organizations and institutions; and the use of specialists to help formulate such plans.[15]

III. Negative and positive features of the policy and its application

As is the case with various other instruments dealing with indigenous peoples' issues, the ADB's Policy on Indigenous Peoples contains positive features or strengths, as well as weaknesses and gaps that could be regarded as the policy's "negative" features.

Weaknesses and negative features

One of the most serious gaps or weaknesses in the policy is the general treatment of the Policy on Indigenous Peoples at par with other policies of the ADB, since it "applies in parallel with and does not replace or supersede other ADB policies and practices".[16] Therefore, theoretically, if there is a contradiction between the ADB's Policy on Indigenous Peoples, another ADB policy or practice, the former (the Policy on Indigenous Peoples) will not necessarily prevail, and this can work to the detriment of indigenous peoples. This was the case, for example, with the ADB's forestry sector support to the Government of Bangladesh, in which the provisions of the ADB's forestry policy prevailed over its Policy on Indigenous Peoples.[17]

In addition, the ADB's other relevant policies and practices must be considered "within the context of national development policies and approaches", since "the fundamental relationship between ADB and governments remains the basis for country-specific operations".[18] In other words, despite provisions in the ADB's Policy on Indigenous Peoples respecting indigenous peoples' rights, needs and concerns, if national development policies and approaches of the borrower country run counter to these, the latter could well defeat, or water down, the impact of the positive aspects of the policy. In fact, this is quite a common occurrence across Asia.

For instance, indigenous peoples on the ground rejected a number of forestry sector legal reforms in Bangladesh because these denied the people's land and resource rights. The

---

[14] Ibid. p. 28 (Appendix).

[15] Ibid.

[16] Ibid. p. 25.

[17] Philip Gain, *Background and Context to the Forest (Amendment) Act, 2000 and the (draft) Social Forestry Rules, 2000*, Society for Environment and Human Development (SEHD), Dhaka, Bangladesh, May 2001, and Raja Devasish Roy and Philip Gain, "Indigenous Peoples and Forests in Bangladesh" in Minority Rights Group (ed.), *Forests and Indigenous Peoples of Asia*, Report 98/4, London, 1999, pp. 21-22.

[18] Ibid.

reforms were facilitated by ADB technical assistance (TA) grants, which are provided in relation to past, ongoing and future loans. Many of the provisions of the national forestry policy of Bangladesh were in conflict with the positive aspects of the ADB's Policy on Indigenous Peoples.[19] Similarly, another ADB-funded social forestry project in Bangladesh, which also affected indigenous peoples, was deemed to have paid little heed to the rights of women.[20]

These examples from Bangladesh illustrate how the differing nature and level of protection provided by the ADB's Policy on Indigenous Peoples and other policies and practices of the ADB can lead to minimal protection of indigenous peoples' rights. Such protection could even verge towards a lowest common denominator situation, rather than strongly and unequivocally upholding the rights of indigenous peoples.

In contrast, the policies addressing indigenous peoples of some non-lending donor institutions, such as the Government of Denmark and the European Commission, provide a far higher status to the rights of indigenous peoples.[21] Of course, one should bear in mind that the Danish government and the European Commission are non-profit institutions. The ADB, although an inter-governmental agency, is managed as a profit-making corporation. Its major decision-making processes are dominated by the strong corporate shareholdings of the different national governments in Asia and other continents.

Strengths and positive features

Despite the weaknesses and gaps of the ADB Indigenous Peoples policy, as mentioned above, a number of other provisions are respectful of the rights of indigenous peoples. These positive provisions have the potential to secure the rights and interests of indigenous peoples, at least in the limited circumstance where the bank and the loanee government are in agreement. The policy states the following:

> "…initiatives should be compatible in substance and structure with the affected peoples' culture and social and economic institutions, and commensurate with the needs, aspirations, and demands of affected peoples. Initiatives should be conceived, planned and implemented, to the maximum extent possible, with the informed consent of affected communities, and include respect for indigenous peoples' dignity, human rights and cultural uniqueness."[22]

Another positive feature of the policy is the acknowledgment of the disadvantaged situation of indigenous peoples. It also refers to international instruments on indigenous peoples' rights and recommends involving and strengthening indigenous peoples' institutions in the Indigenous Peoples Development Plan.[23]

---

[19] Raja Devasish Roy and Sadeka Halim, "A Critique to the Forest (Amendment) Act of 2000 and the (draft) Social Forestry Rules of 2000", published by the Society for Environment and Human Development (SEHD), Dhaka, Bangladesh, May 2001. Philip Gain, *Background and Context to the Forest (Amendment) Act, 2000 and the (draft) Social Forestry Rules, 2000*, Society for Environment and Human Development (SEHD), Dhaka, Bangladesh, May 2001.

[20] Sadeka Halim, "Social Forestry in Bangladesh and the Role of Women" in *Discourse: A Journal of Policy Studies*, Vol. 3, Number 2, Winter 1999, Institute for Development Policy Analysis and Advocacy, Proshika, Dhaka, pp. 58-79.

[21] See, respectively, (i) *Danish Strategy for Indigenous Peoples* and (ii) Working Document of the [European] Commission of May 1998.

[22] Asian Development Bank, *Policy on Indigenous Peoples*, p., 17.

[23] Ibid. pp. 13-15.

Difficulties, however, lie in the process of implementation. The ADB does not provide parallel mechanisms to ensure that the previously mentioned positive provisions are regarded as mandatory. A similar situation prevails in the case of the World Bank's policy on indigenous peoples, which bears striking similarities with the ADB's. Recent reforms to the World Bank's policy on indigenous peoples – the replacement of OD 4.20 by OP 4.10/BP 4.10 – include many desirable provisions that respect indigenous peoples' rights. However, these appear to be merely recommendatory, rather than mandatory.[24]

Well-researched and objective findings on the positive impacts of ADB-funded development programmes on indigenous peoples are hard to find. The scarce literature that show ADB interventions in indigenous peoples' areas in a positive light appear to have been initiated or facilitated by the ADB itself. In Bangladesh, for example, ADB-funded projects are generally regarded as harmful rather than beneficial to indigenous peoples.[25] Nevertheless, the possibility of positive and creative use of the policy to safeguard indigenous peoples' rights and interests should not be ruled out.

IV. Case study: ADB project intervention for indigenous people, the Chittagong Hill Tracts Rural Development Project

A *potentially* positive example of ADB intervention, with support from the indigenous people of the area concerned, is the Chittagong Hill Tracts Rural Development Project in Bangladesh.[26] The project was initiated with the consent of the Chittagong Hill Tracts Regional Council, the premier indigenous-majority semi-autonomous institution of the Chittagong Hill Tracts region. The project includes the indigenous chairperson of this council as the *ex-officio* chairperson of the project's Regional Coordination Committee, with three indigenous district council chairpersons and the three traditional paramount chiefs as members.[27] The project's primary focus is to reduce "absolute poverty" in the Chittagong Hill Tracts region and to provide a confidence-building environment to underpin the Chittagong Hill Tracts Peace Accord of 1997. The project also includes a Community Development component with programmes on legal literacy, training and gender.[28] The

---

[24] See, for example, statement of representative of Indigenous Peoples' Organizations participating at the Round Table meeting on the World Bank's Indigenous Peoples' Policy in Washington, D.C., USA on 17 October 2002.

[25] See, e.g., (i) Philip Gain, *The Last Forests of Bangladesh*, Society for Environment and Human Development, Dhaka, February 1998 (esp. pp. 151-174) and (ii) Suhas Chakma, "ADB Programs in Bangladesh: Identifying the Critical Issues", in Indigenous Perspectives: A Journal of the Tebtebba Foundation, Vol. III, Number 1, Baguio City, Philippines, 2000, pp. 140-150.

[26] This project was initiated through ADB Loan No. 1771-BAN (SF). The project commenced in May 2004 and is scheduled for completion in March 2008. See, e.g., *Project Proforma of the Ministry of Chittagong Hill Tracts Affairs, Government of Bangladesh, March, 2004* and SMEC International Pty Ltd, *Chittagong Hill Tracts Rural Development Project: Second Consultant Report to the CHT Regional Coordination Committee*, 13 July 2005.

[27] Project Proforma of the Ministry of Chittagong Hill Tracts Affairs, Government of Bangladesh, March 2004, p. 67 (Annex 20).

[28] SMEC International Pty Ltd, *Chittagong Hill Tracts Rural Development Project*: Second Consultant Report to the CHT Regional Coordination Committee, 13 July 2005, pp. 7-14.

loan agreement between the ADB and the Government of Bangladesh refers to the monitoring and implementation of an Indigenous Peoples Development Plan by the project-monitoring unit.[29]

The involvement of representative institutions of indigenous peoples in decision-making and project implementation is no doubt a desirable development, if that has happened with the prior, informed consent of the peoples concerned. However, the potentially positive impact of the project is at risk of being diluted, or even undone, by certain features of the project that have been included without the knowledge and consent of the peoples concerned. In particular, the inclusion into the project of micro-credit disbursement by local NGOs was apparently done at the behest of the ADB's president rather than by the wishes of the indigenous peoples of the region.[30] At a recent meeting of the Regional Coordination Committee, serious concerns were raised by the chairperson and other indigenous members regarding the proposed loan disbursement, which is in violation of regional laws, practices and interests of local indigenous people.[31]

V. Monitoring, evaluation and policy review

An important factor in ensuring the implementation of the positive features of the ADB's Policy on Indigenous Peoples is effective monitoring. This, in turn, is dependent on the ADB's internal mechanisms and processes of monitoring and evaluation, as well as on the external processes of monitoring and evaluation by indigenous peoples, governments and NGOs.

With regard to internal monitoring, the ADB's most important agencies are the Office of Environment and Social Development, the Programmes Department (in relation to country programming), the resident missions in the countries, and the Operations Evaluation Office, the last-named being involved predominantly in "post-evaluation" functions.[32] However, it appears that these agencies do not have much influence on the ADB's operations in areas inhabited by indigenous peoples, except in limited circumstances such as the project in the Chittagong Hill Tracts region in Bangladesh.

In the case of the Office of Environment and Social Development, individual employees may have the required attitude and respect for indigenous peoples' rights, aspirations and perspectives. However, their views seem to run counter to those of other weightier

---

[29] Agreement on Loan No. 1771 BAN (SF) on the *Chittagong Hill Tracts Rural Development Project* between the People's Republic of Bangladesh and the Asian Development Bank, dated, 18 December 2000 (esp. Schedule 6, paragraph 30).

[30] *Report and Recommendation of the President to the Board of Directors on a Proposed Loan to the People's Republic of Bangladesh for the Chittagong Hill Tracts Rural Development Project (RRP: BAN 32467)*, Asian Development Bank, October, 2000, p. 16 (paragraphs 46, 47).

[31] 5th meeting of Regional Coordination Committee of the Chittagong Hill Tracts Rural Development Project, held in Rangamati, Chittagong Hill Tracts, Bangladesh on 4 July 2005, attended by the writer (in his capacity as a member of the committee by virtue of being one of the chiefs of the region). The local NGO, Taungya, withdrew its application to be included among the local NGOs to help implement the project when it realized that it would have to also engage in a micro-credit operation by investing its own funds (in addition to subsidies from the government); interview with Amlan Chakma, Executive Director, Taungya, Rangamati, Bangladesh, 25 October 2005.

[32] Asian Development Bank, *Policy on Indigenous Peoples*, p., 24.

2

departments and agencies within the ADB. The situation is best illustrated by a comment made informally by a World Bank employee. He lamented, "What can we, a dozen or so sociologists and anthropologists, do in the wake of contrary views of our more influential economist colleagues, whose numbers run into the hundreds, and whose primary concerns have little to do with the welfare of indigenous peoples or other such groups…"[33]

In any future revision of ADB's Policy on Indigenous Peoples, the findings of the ADB Operations Evaluation Office, if obtained in an accurate and objective manner, would be of great assistance. In the case of the World Bank, the ADB ignored or missed a similar opportunity to disseminate and utilize the findings of its corresponding agency, the Operations Evaluation Department, during appropriate stages of its Indigenous Peoples' Policy revision process.[34] Therefore, a crucial factor in determining proper implementation, monitoring and evaluation, and consequent revision, is the question of how participatory the ADB's approach is in involving indigenous peoples in the relevant processes.

Opportunities can always be created to open the necessary space for indigenous perspectives, if the ADB's high-level decision-makers can muster the will to do so. The ADB has formally consulted indigenous peoples and other "stakeholders" in the process of policy-formulation,[35] and policy-review in certain cases.[36] However, these processes are generally inadequate in terms of time and opportunity given to indigenous peoples and other stakeholders to provide their inputs.[37] Only a few of these processes were sufficiently inclusive or transparent.[38] Unless such trends are corrected, indigenous peoples will remain substantively deprived of their rights in ADB-financed projects and interventions in their areas.

The example of the World Bank's consultation process for its recently reformed indigenous peoples' policy was one of inadequate consultation and sensitivity.[39] The experience suggests that indigenous peoples need to strengthen their lobbying efforts if they are to influence reforms in policy and practice of multilateral development banks in the right direction. It would do well to remember that, ultimately, institutions such as the ADB and the World Bank are primarily oriented towards profit. Their perspective of economic growth through "poverty reduction" is insufficiently receptive of indigenous perspectives on rights and development.

---

[33] This comment was made in the presence of this writer, some years ago in an international meeting related to indigenous peoples' rights by a World Bank official, whose identity it would not be right to divulge without consent.

[34] *Statement of Indigenous Participants at the Consultation on the World Bank's Draft Policy on Indigenous Peoples* (OP/BP 4.10), Dhaka, Bangladesh, 14 November 2001, attended by this writer.

[35] For example, the ADB held one formal consultation with indigenous peoples' representatives regarding its (then draft) *Policy on Indigenous Peoples* in Punta Baluarte, Philippines in 1995 (which was also attended by this writer).

[36] For example, the *Regional Workshop on Review of the Asian Development Bank's Forestry Policy* held in Manila, Philippines, on 14-15 February 2002 (attended by this writer).

[37] For example, in the case of the draft *Policy on Indigenous Peoples* meeting held in Punta Baluarte, Philippines, 1995.

[38] For example, at the *Regional Workshop on Review of the Asian Development Bank's Forestry Policy* held in Manila on 14-15 February 2002, this writer was perhaps among only one or two participants who criticized the draft policy, with the overwhelming majority of participants remaining either silent or making non-critical remarks about the draft. This writer concluded, therefore, that this was substantively an orchestrated meeting that consciously excluded critical voices. This is also the opinion of Chris Lang in "ADB's Draft Forest Policy: The Politics of Participation", published in *WRM Bulletin* 74, September 2003.

[39] See, for example, the statement of representative of Indigenous Peoples' Organizations participating at the Round Table meeting on the World Bank's Indigenous Peoples' Policy held in *Washington, D.C., USA* on 17 October 2002 (attended by this writer).

Despite such limitations, indigenous peoples can strengthen their networking and organizational skills and help steer policy reforms in their hoped-for direction through advocacy, lobbying and policy dialogue. With this as a backdrop, a number of observations are made below, which can facilitate indigenous peoples' efforts to change the relevant policies and practices of the ADB. This change is necessary in order to bring the policies and practices of the ADB in conformity with existing and emerging international standards on the rights of indigenous peoples.

VI. Conclusions: Ways forward

Reform the existing policy

There is much room to improve upon the contents of the ADB's Policy on Indigenous Peoples. The current policy accounts for the rights of indigenous peoples, without an unequivocal commitment to honour and respect these rights. More importantly, the policy does not provide adequate mechanisms to adhere to such rights. The basic rights of indigenous peoples, including their right to self-determination, their rights over their lands and territories, and their right to prior and informed consent[40] concerning development interventions in their areas are now part of customary international law. These need to be unequivocally acknowledged as part of mandatory guidelines in any policy revision.

Process of review and reform

Although the ADB did consult a limited number of indigenous peoples' representatives prior to the adoption of its current Policy on Indigenous Peoples, such consultations were regarded by indigenous peoples as inadequate.[41] The process of reforming the ADB's Forestry policy, for example, was seriously flawed by being insufficiently open, transparent or inclusive.[42] Similarly to be avoided is the manner in which the World Bank held formal consultations with indigenous peoples' representatives, including legal experts, between 2002-2005.[43] The modalities for a future review process of the ADB Policy on Indigenous Peoples need to be agreed upon, with input from indigenous peoples. Such consultations need to be preceded by an in-depth evaluation of the diverse impacts of ADB-funded projects on indigenous peoples.

---

[40] In its new policy on indigenous peoples (OP 4.10), the World Bank mentioned the requirement of Prior Informed *Consultation*, which has been rejected by indigenous peoples since it falls short of the principle of Prior Informed *Consent*.

[41] This writer was among the participants at a formal consultation on the policy held at Punta Baluarte, Philippines, in 1995. Many of the participants at the meeting felt that the process of consultations was not participatory enough and therefore advised the ADB's representatives to hold further formal consultations with indigenous peoples' representatives. This advice does not seem to have been accepted or acted upon by the ADB.

[42] See for example, Chris Lang in "ADB's Draft Forest Policy: The Politics of Participation", published in *WRM Bulletin* 74, September 2003.

[43] This is noted in a letter written by representatives of indigenous peoples to the Vice Chairman of the World Bank, on 24 March 2004, expressing concern over the process of consultations.

Monitoring and evaluation of project impact upon indigenous peoples

The experience of the European Commission (EC) in having some of its projects evaluated by indigenous experts, and the findings shared among indigenous peoples and EC project staff and policy-level officials, can provide ideas for similar evaluation exercises of ADB-funded projects. Indigenous peoples have demanded that the World Bank involve local, national and regional indigenous organizations in actively tracking and monitoring its operations throughout the whole project cycle.[44] Such needs are equally relevant in the case of the ADB.

Influencing policy reforms by ADB member country governments

Since the ADB's Policy on Indigenous Peoples is affected by the relevant policies of the borrower governments, the positive impact of the ADB's policy would be watered down or countered in the absence of adequate acknowledgement of indigenous peoples' rights in national laws and policies. Some have advocated that the ADB engage the concerned national governments to initiate policy reforms in their countries and to effectively implement the ADB's Policy on Indigenous Peoples.[45] It is important in this respect to encourage ADB country member governments to not only consult indigenous peoples, but to institutionalize appropriate methods of consultation.[46]

Disseminating data and information

Dissemination of data and information (in appropriate forms) is crucial to ensuring that the necessary implementation and reform process is in accordance with the rights of indigenous peoples. This can also promote transparency and accountability.[47]

Including indigenous peoples in bank-member country negotiations

The ADB policy clearly declares that "the fundamental relationship between the ADB and governments remains the basis for country-specific operations".[48] Indigenous peoples are, however, often unaware of the contractual relationship between the ADB and borrower governments. This problem needs to be corrected through indigenous participation, both in the deliberations of the ADB and in policy dialogues with the concerned government.[49]

---

[44] Statement of representative of Indigenous Peoples' Organizations participating at a Round Table meeting on the World Bank's Indigenous Peoples' Policy held in Washington, D.C., USA on 17 October 2002.

[45] Suhas Chakma, "ADB Programs in Bangladesh: Identifying the Critical Issues", in *Indigenous Perspectives: A Journal of the Tebtebba Foundation*, Vol. III, Number 1, Baguio City, Philippines, 2000, pp. 140-173, at p. 149.

[46] Raja Devasish Roy, "Perspectives of Indigenous Peoples on the Review of the Asian Development Bank's Forest Policy", paper presented at the *Regional Workshop on Review of the Asian Development Bank's Forestry Policy* held in Manila, Philippines, on 14-15 February 2002.

[47] Ibid. See also, Suhas Chakma, op. cit., p. 148.

[48] Asian Development Bank, *Policy on Indigenous Peoples*, p. 25.

[49] Statement of representative of Indigenous Peoples' Organizations participating at a *Round Table* meeting on the World Bank's Indigenous Peoples' Policy held in Washington, DC, USA on 17 October 2002.

Sources

Papers and articles

Chakma, Suhas, 2000. "ADB Programs in Bangladesh: Identifying the Critical Issues", in *Indigenous Perspectives: A Journal of the Tebtebba Foundation*, Vol. III, Number 1, Baguio City, Philippines, 2000, pp. 140-173.

Gain, Philip, 1998. *The Last Forests of Bangladesh*, Society for Environment and Human Development (SEHD), Dhaka, February 1998 (esp. pp. 151-174).

Gain, Philip, 2001. *Background and Context to the Forest (Amendment) Act, 2000 and the (draft) Social Forestry Rules, 2000*, Society for Environment and Human Development (SEHD), Dhaka, Bangladesh, May 2001.

Halim, Sadeka, 1999. "Social Forestry in Bangladesh and the Role of Women" in *Discourse: A Journal of Policy Studies*, Vol. 3, Number 2, Winter 1999, Institute for Development Policy Analysis and Advocacy, Proshika, Dhaka, pp. 58-79.

Lang, Chris, 2003. "ADB's Draft Forest Policy: The Politics of Participation", published in *WRM Bulletin* 74, September 2003.

Minority Rights Group (ed.), *Forests and Indigenous Peoples of Asia*, Report 98/4, London, 1999.

Roy, Raja Devasish, 2002. "Perspectives of Indigenous Peoples on the Review of the Asian Development Bank's Forest Policy", paper presented at the *Regional Workshop on Review of the Asian Development Bank's Forestry Policy* held in Manila, Philippines, on 14-15 February 2002.

_____ and Philip Gain, 1999. "Indigenous Peoples and Forests in Bangladesh" in Minority Rights Group (ed.), *Forests and Indigenous Peoples of Asia*, Report 98/4, London, 1999, pp. 21-22.

_____ and Sadeka Halim, 2001. "A Critique to the Forest (Amendment) Act of 2000 and (Draft) Social Forestry Rules of 2000", published by Society for Environment and Human Development (SEHD), Dhaka, Bangladesh, May 2001.

2

Other Documents

Asian Development Bank, 1998. *Policy on Indigenous Peoples*, Manila, Philippines.

_____, 2000. *Report and Recommendation of the President to the Board of Directors on a Proposed Loan to the People's Republic of Bangladesh for the Chittagong Hill Tracts Rural Development Project (RRP: BAN 32467)*, Asian Development Bank, October, 2000.

European Commission, 1998. *Working Document of the [European] Commission of May 1998*.

Ministry of Chittagong Hill Tracts Affairs, 2004. *Project Proforma for Chittagong Hill Tracts Rural Development Project*, Ministry of Chittagong Hill Tracts Affairs, Government of Bangladesh, March 2004.

Ministry of Foreign Affairs, Government of Denmark, 1998. *Danish Strategy for Indigenous Peoples*.

SMEC International Pty Ltd, 2005. *Chittagong Hill Tracts Rural Development Project: Second Consultant Report to the CHT Regional Coordination Committee*, 13 July 2005.

World Bank, Operational Directive 4.20, Operational Policy 4.10, Bank Procedure 4.10.

3

Japan Bank for International Cooperation Guidelines for Confirmation of Environmental and Social Considerations: Implications on Indigenous Peoples

Joan Carling
Friends of the Earth-Japan

I. Institutional review

The Japan Bank for International Cooperation, or JBIC, is the second largest development bank in the world. It was established in 1999 when two large Japanese financial institutions merged, the Japan Export-Import Bank (JEXIM) and the Overseas Economic Cooperation Fund (OECF).

OECF was mainly responsible for providing Yen Loans, one type of Official Development Assistance (ODA). According to the Japanese Government, the purpose of Yen Loans is to promote the economic development and welfare of developing countries. JEXIM did other kinds of International Financial Operations (IFOs) that were not ODA loans, such as export loans, import loans, investment loans, and untied loans. The purpose of IFOs is to support Japanese companies' exports and investments.

Because JBIC was established by putting these two institutions together, it now is responsible for both Yen Loans as well as the IFOs. JBIC therefore lends to governments of developing countries and also to Japanese and foreign companies.

JBIC finances projects worldwide. Most of the projects it finances, however, are in Asia. Of all Yen Loans, approximately 80 percent are given to countries in Asia. About 7 percent of Yen Loans are to countries in Africa, 6.5 percent to Latin and South America, 4.3 percent to the Middle East and 0.8 percent elsewhere (based on the data of FY 2002). As of the end of 2003, JBIC had outstanding loans of US$192.3 billion and annual lending of US $17.7 billion. There are 40 countries receiving loans from JBIC.

JBIC has focused its financing on large-scale infrastructure projects. While some of these projects have contributed to the development of certain areas, a very significant number of its funded projects, particularly large infrastructure projects, have caused a lot of damage to the environment. These include air and water pollution, damaged ecosystems and the loss of biodiversity in many parts of the world. Affected people have also suffered significantly due to projects financed by JBIC. This has been due to involuntary resettlements, loss of livelihood and negative consequences on the socio-cultural life of the people. Destruction of ecosystems has also made living a traditional lifestyle impossible. It has divided communities and destroyed cultures. Compensation for damages to those adversely affected has not been sufficient and their lives have further deteriorated. Those who have suffered most from ill-conceived projects funded by JBIC are the poor, women, children, the elderly and indigenous peoples.

JBIC is largely funding projects in Asia where most indigenous peoples are found, thus, more and more indigenous peoples are adversely affected by JBIC-funded projects. Experience has shown the dire consequences of JBIC-funded projects on the recognition of the collective rights, interest and welfare of indigenous peoples. Indigenous peoples are time and again made to sacrifice for "development," as though their existence could be traded with modernity and progress usually associated with the expropriation, exploitation and destruction of their land and resources.

II. JBIC environmental and social guidelines

JBIC established a new set of environmental and social guidelines in April 2002, entitled "JBIC Guidelines for Confirmation of Environmental and Social Considerations (the Guidelines)." The new guidelines were the result of extensive lobby work done by Japanese NGOs, in partnership with NGOs in developing countries, including organizations of indigenous peoples. Substantial recommendations pertaining to social issues and human rights, drawn from community lessons and experiences with JBIC-funded projects, were submitted to JBIC for incorporation in the new guidelines. However, these recommendations were not reflected in the new set of guidelines. Nevertheless, the new Guidelines are much better and more encompassing than the old ones. The new Guidelines put more emphasis on environment protection and procedures on environmental and social considerations for project funding and monitoring.

The preface of the Guidelines states that:

> Japan Bank for International Cooperation (hereafter referred to as "JBIC") establishes and makes public "JBIC Guidelines for Confirmation of Environmental and Social Considerations" (hereafter referred to as the "Guidelines") with the objective of contributing to efforts by the international community, particularly developing regions, towards sustainable development, through consideration of the environmental and social aspects in all projects (hereafter referred to as "projects") subject to lending or other financial operations (hereafter referred to as "funding") by JBIC. Environmental and social considerations refer not only to the natural environment, but also to social issues such as involuntary resettlement and respect for human rights of indigenous peoples (hereafter collectively referred to as "environment"). The guidelines apply commonly to JBIC's International Financial Operations and Overseas Economic Cooperation Operations.[1]

The first part of the Guidelines[2] contains basic policies, principles and procedures and disclosure of information for confirmation of environmental and social considerations. It also includes environmental reviews for decision-making and loan agreements, as well as compliance with guidelines and implementation and review of guidelines.

The second part[3] deals with environmental and social considerations required for funding projects, categorization of projects, information required for the screening process, and items requiring monitoring. The section on environmental and social considerations for funding contains provisions on compliance with laws, standards and plans; social acceptability and social impacts; involuntary resettlement, indigenous peoples and monitoring.

Because the Guidelines are new, its implementation is only for new projects for which funds were requested on or after 1 October 2003, which was when its effectively commenced.

---

[1] Japan Bank for International Cooperation, *JBIC Guidelines for Confirmation of Environmental and Social Considerations*, p.1.

[2] Ibid. pp. 3-12.

[3] Ibid. pp. 13-25.

JBIC has also established Objection Procedures under the new Guidelines.[4] This mechanism is for project-affected people to file a compliant to JBIC if they have reasons or basis to believe that JBIC has not followed its own Guidelines. A complaint sent through the objection procedures will then be given to a neutral Examiner appointed by JBIC who will review and investigate the complaint.

Since the Guidelines were written in a comprehensive manner and not with separate specific guidelines on key areas for environment and social consideration, there is only one provision pertaining specifically to indigenous peoples. Some of the other provisions are also relevant to indigenous peoples as enumerated below:

The Guidelines: Part 2.1 Environmental and Social Considerations Required for Funded Projects

(Indigenous Peoples)

- When a project may have adverse impact on indigenous peoples, all of their rights in relation to land and resources must be respected in accordance with the spirit of the relevant international declarations and treaties. Efforts must be made to obtain the consent of indigenous peoples after they have been fully informed.[5]

(Involuntary Resettlement)

- Involuntary resettlement and loss of means of livelihood are to be avoided where feasible, exploring all viable alternatives. When after such examination, it is proved unfeasible, effective measures to minimize impact and to compensate for losses must be agreed upon with people who will be affected;

- People who must be resettled involuntarily and people whose means of livelihood will be hindered or lost must be sufficiently compensated and supported by project proponents, etc. in a timely manner. The project proponents, etc. must make efforts to enable people affected by the project to improve their standard of living, income opportunities and production levels. Measures to achieve this may include: providing land and monetary compensation of losses (to cover land and property losses), supporting the means for alternative sustainable livelihood and providing the expenses necessary for relocation and the re-establishment of a community at relocation sites; and

- Appropriate participation by the people affected and their communities must be promoted in planning, implementation and monitoring of involuntary resettlement, loss of their means of livelihood, plans and measures against it.[6]

---

[4] Japan Bank for International Cooperation. *Summary of Procedures to Submit Objections Concerning JBIC Guidelines for Confirmation of Environmental and Social Considerations.*

[5] Japan Bank for International Cooperation. *JBIC Guidelines for Confirmation of Environmental and Social Considerations,* p.15.

[6] Ibid.

Indigenous Peoples and the Human Rights-Based Approach to Development

(Social Acceptability and Social Impacts)

- Projects must be adequately coordinated so that they are accepted in a manner that is socially appropriate to the country and locality in which the project is planned. For projects with potentially large environmental impacts, sufficient consultations with stakeholders, such as local residents, must be conducted vis disclosure of information from an early stage where alternative proposals for the project plan may be examined. The outcome of such consultations must be incorporated into the contents of the project; and

- Appropriate consideration must be given to vulnerable social groups, such as women, children, the elderly, the poor, and ethnic minorities, all of whom are susceptible to environmental and social impacts and who may have little access to the decision-making process within society.[7]

(Monitoring)

- When third parties point out, in concrete terms, that environmental and social considerations are not being fully undertaken, it is desirable that a forum for discussion and examination of countermeasures can be established based on sufficient information disclosure and include the participation of stakeholders in the relevant project. It is also desirable that an agreement be reached on procedures to be adopted with a view to resolving the problem.[8]

III. How do the new guidelines relate to collective rights of indigenous peoples and to social issues?

While there are positive provisions of the JBIC Guidelines relating to indigenous peoples and to social considerations, these are by far very inadequate in ensuring the respect and recognition of indigenous peoples' rights and fundamental human rights pertaining to development concerns. The provision on indigenous peoples, which mentions the respect of IP rights in relation to land and resources in accordance with the spirit of relevant international declarations and treaties, does not provide the substance and mechanisms to ensure the implementation of this provision.

Provision on indigenous peoples

The single provision addressing the collective rights of indigenous peoples[9] does not comprehensively capture the particularities of indigenous peoples as one of the groups most vulnerable to development interventions with long-term adverse impacts. It does not account for the interrelationship of land and resources to the indigenous peoples' distinct ways of life, identity and culture, and indigenous socio-political systems. Further, it does not recognize the indigenous peoples' collective views and concept on the use and

---

[7] Ibid. pp. 14, 15.

[8] Ibid. p. 16.

[9] Ibid. p. 15.

management of land and resources, commonly targeted for "development". Thus, the provision for the respect of the rights of indigenous peoples in relation to land and resources becomes shallow as there is no further elaboration of this right. Protecting the distinct ways of life of indigenous peoples, their culture and identity as well as their collective integrity, should be part of their sustainable development, as a matter of their right to self-determination.

The provision that "efforts must be made to obtain the consent of the indigenous peoples after they have been fully informed"[10] is too weak, as it does not require "consent" of affected indigenous peoples for projects applied for funding by JBIC. This is contrary to existing international standards on the recognition of the right to "Free Prior and Informed Consent" or "FPIC", in relation to indigenous peoples.

"Observing that indigenous peoples have suffered and continue to suffer from discrimination", and, "in particular that they have lost their land and resources to colonists, commercial companies and State enterprises," the Committee on the Elimination of Racial Discrimination called upon states-parties to "ensure that members of indigenous peoples have equal rights in respect of effective participation in public life, and that no decisions directly relating to their rights and interests are taken without their informed consent."[i]

The UN Committee on Economic, Social and Cultural Rights in 2001, noted "with regret that the traditional lands of indigenous peoples have been reduced or occupied, without their consent, by timber, mining and oil companies, at the expense of the exercise of their culture and the equilibrium of the ecosystem." It then recommended that the state "ensure the participation of indigenous peoples in decisions affecting their lives. The Committee particularly urges the State party to consult and seek the consent of the indigenous peoples concerned…"[ii]

Other international bodies that have accepted the right of indigenous peoples to FPIC include the following:

- UN Sub-Commission on Promotion and Protection of Human Rights
- UN Permanent Forum on Indigenous Issues
- UN Working Group on Indigenous Populations
- UN Development Programme
- UN Centre for Transnational Corporations
- Convention on Biological Diversity
- Convention to Combat Desertification, particularly in Africa
- Inter-American Commission on Human Rights
- Inter-American Development Bank
- Andean Community
- European Council of Ministers

[10] Ibid. p. 15.

- European Commission

- Organization of African Unity

Given the level of international acceptance of the right of indigenous peoples to FPIC, the JBIC Guidelines then lacks the requirement for the recognition and respect of FPIC, which is very critical in addressing the concerns of indigenous peoples with regard to development intervention. The fear that FPIC gives "veto rights" to indigenous peoples overshadows the fundamental premise that the participation of indigenous peoples in the decision-making process is within the framework of their right to self- determination.

Other provisions of the Guidelines on requirements for project funding, such as social acceptability and social impacts,[11] resettlement[12] and project monitoring,[13] contain positive measures that could be useful for indigenous peoples. These are the requirements on disclosure of information, sufficient consultation and alternative proposals with less environment impacts, sufficient compensation for resettled people, and appropriate participation by affected people in the planning, implementation and monitoring of involuntary resettlement plans. However, there are major loopholes in these provisions in relation to the concrete measures and mechanisms that could ensure the exercise of the rights of affected communities, including indigenous peoples.

Information disclosure

On the provision for information disclosure,[14] this will be mainly done through the website of JBIC[15], and some documents will only be in Japanese. Therefore, there are serious problems in terms of access to information by affected communities, especially remote communities. Understanding these documents is another problem because documents for disclosure are either in Japanese and English only, and not in a language affected communities are familiar with. Likewise, JBIC upholds the confidentiality of certain information in relation to commercial and other matters. Some of this information is also important for the affected communities and the public to know, especially if it pertains to the terms of agreement which may be disadvantageous to the borrower and the public.

The positive aspect of JBIC's information disclosure guideline is the right of affected communities and other stakeholders to inform JBIC of their views, concerns and position in relation to a project under application to JBIC for their consideration. However, it does not mention how this information will be considered in the decision-making process of JBIC.

Involuntary resettlement

While the JBIC Guidelines provide for 'alternative options' to avoid involuntary resettlement if possible,[16] the bank still considers funding projects which will lead to involuntary

---

[11] Ibid. pp. 14, 15.

[12] Ibid. p. 15.

[13] Ibid. p. 16.

[14] Ibid. pp. 9, 10.

[15] Japan Bank for International Cooperation, *http://www.jbic.go.jp/english/environ/joho/index.php*

[16] Ibid. p. 15.

resettlement. One of the most critical, irreversible, long-lasting and adverse impacts of development projects on indigenous peoples is involuntary resettlement. Indigenous peoples' culture, identity, survival and development are very much tied up with their land and resources. Thus, the displacement of indigenous peoples from their land and resources does not only imply economic dislocation but also disruption of the socio-cultural dimension of their survival as indigenous peoples. For indigenous peoples, "Land is life." Thus, involuntary resettlement, as provided in the JBIC Guidelines, is a direct violation of indigenous peoples' right to land and resources. This provision for involuntary resettlement is contradictory to the other provision of the JBIC Guidelines pertaining to the "respect for the right of indigenous peoples in relation to their land and resources." [17]

On the provision for compensation for the loss of land and property, to include monetary compensation, land and livelihood[18], these compensation measures cannot replace the loss of indigenous peoples in terms of the socio-cultural impacts of displacement. These impacts are beyond material compensation thereby requiring more thorough social impact studies that must be taken into account in the decision-making process of JBIC.

Social acceptability and impacts

The JBIC guidelines on social acceptability and social impacts mention the positive requirement for sufficient consultation and information disclosure.[19] However, these fall short of the right to FPIC of affected indigenous communities as already mentioned above. The right to FPIC is by far the most appropriate mechanism for social acceptability of projects by indigenous peoples. The substance and mechanism of FPIC does not only relate to information disclosure, but also provides for the right of communities to receive information in a language understood by them, and to request other related and relevant information from other sources. Likewise, the right to FPIC does not only provide for consultations, but rather, consent that is freely given, not under coercion, bribery or duress. Also under FPIC, indigenous systems of decision-making are recognized. The FPIC provision is by far the most appropriate mechanism for social acceptability of projects by indigenous peoples.

Monitoring

While JBIC allows the formation of a forum to include stakeholders in addressing environmental and social impacts of projects under implementation,[20] it fails to provide for a clear mechanism of accountability by project proponents and funders. Experience has shown that outstanding issues in relation to environmental and social impacts of JBIC-funded projects remain unresolved.

Objection Procedure

While the Objection Procedure is a positive step in addressing possible violations by JBIC of its own Guidelines, there is no clear mechanism on how these violations will be addressed

---

[17] Ibid. p. 15.

[18] Ibid. p. 15.

[19] Ibid. pp. 14, 15.

[20] Ibid. p. 16.

by JBIC and what affected communities can expect in terms of compensation and redress of grievances. The only defined process in the Objection Procedure is the appointment of an independent/neutral Examiner[21] who will receive the complaint, evaluate it, conduct his/her own independent investigation and submit a report and recommendation to the Governor.[22] It is then up to the Governor to decide what to do with the report and recommendation. Thus, there still is no clear accountability on the part of JBIC for proven violations of its own Guidelines.

IV. Brief history of indigenous engagement with or opposition to JBIC

Koto Panjang Dam, Indonesia (1992–96)

The Koto Panjang Dam on the Kampar Kanan and Mahat Rivers in West Sumatra, Indonesia, was built with loans from what is now the Japan Bank for International Cooperation (JBIC). The feasibility study for the project was funded by the Japan International Cooperation Agency (JICA) and carried out by the Tokyo Electric Power Services Co., Ltd (TEPSCO). Japanese and Indonesian companies were awarded the construction contracts for the main part of the dam.

At least 4,886 households, representing between 17,000 and 23,000 people, were relocated in the early 1990s to make way for the dam. Those displaced by the dam were Minagkabau, who lived according to their traditional customs and culture. The Minagkabau are an ethnic group living mainly in West Sumatra province, in the midwestern part of the island of Sumatra. The Minagkabau consist of village communities based on customary law. They are followers of Islam, and there is a mosque and a communal building called the *rumah gadang* (meaning "large house") at the center of every village. Land in Minagkabau society is traditionally communally owned, with each village having common land (*ulayat*) for use by the entire village or an individual clan (*suku*). The *ulayat* cannot be bought and sold, and is guided by customary law.

The project's feasibility study failed to take into account any of these characteristics of Minagkabau society. The evictees mounted a strong resistance to the treatment they were receiving, but the Suharto regime stationed military in the area and suppressed the opposition. Thus, with the social and cultural identity of Minagkabau society ignored, the villagers were resettled in a place that had neither *ulayat* nor a *rumah gadang*. In addition, housing provided by the government was not the traditional Minagkabau style on stilts, but rather poorly-built wooden houses situated directly on the ground. Problems arose with the newly built mosques as well, with some were facing the wrong direction and others too small for everyone to enter, so that the people had to build their own mosques. Besides these problems, existing relationships in society were ruined when people lost respect for some village leaders who had difficulty coping with resettlement and accepted bribes.

---

[21] Japan Bank for International Cooperation. *Summary of Procedures to Submit Objections Concerning JBIC Guidelines for Confirmation of Environmental and Social Considerations*, p.4.

[22] Ibid. pp. 9-14.

small for everyone to enter, so that the people had to build their own mosques. Besides these problems, existing relationships in society were ruined when people lost respect for some village leaders who had difficulty coping with resettlement and accepted bribes.

The Minagkabau traditional lifestyle and culture has been destroyed and their living standards have declined considerably. The local people had demanded a halt to the dam construction and Japanese funding from the time that work started in 1992. However, their pleas were ignored and the project was completed in 1996. Nevertheless, the voices of opposition have continued to this day. In September 2002, 3,861 people from the project area filed a lawsuit in the Tokyo District Court demanding that the Japanese government, JBIC, JICA and TEPSCO take measures to restore the affected rivers, and that they pay compensation of 5 million yen (about $42,000) per person.

San Roque Dam, Philippines (1998–2003)

The San Roque Multi-purpose Project has been one of the most controversial projects funded by JBIC to date. The dam has displaced more than 4,400 people, and threatens the livelihood of thousands of indigenous Ibaloi people living upstream of the dam.

The Agno River is known as the cultural heartland of the Ibaloi people. The fertile lands along the river and the gold ore found in the mountains have sustained several distinct Ibaloi communities engaged in agriculture, fishing and small-scale gold panning for generations. For the Ibaloi, land and water are resources to be used and shared with their kin, ancestors and gods. These very resources are under threat because of the San Roque Dam project. The Cordillera People's Alliance estimates that approximately 20,000 residents of Itogon, Benguet, will be affected by sediment that will accumulate behind the reservoir over the course of the dam's life. This sediment will eventually submerge the homes, rice terraces, orchards, pasture lands, gardens and burial grounds of the Ibaloi living close to the Agno River.

This is not the first time the Ibaloi have experienced the negative impacts of hydroelectric dams. The Ambuklao and Binga dams were constructed upstream along the Agno River in the 1950s. During that time, the Ibaloi were called upon to sacrifice their lands and their lives for the sake of "national development". Though both dams were for electric power, nearby communities have seen few benefits and most still have no electricity. Many of those relocated were never compensated for the loss of their homes, lands and livelihoods, and more than 70 Ibaloi families lost their land and houses to sedimentation that has backed up behind the Ambuklao Dam. At present, Ambuklao Dam is non-functional as a result of the serious sedimentation problem. Binga Dam is also heavily silted and its partial operation is maintained by the water coming from Ambuklao Dam. Because of this experience, the Ibaloi have been opposed to the San Roque Dam project even before its inception in 1998.

The Indigenous Peoples' Rights Act (IPRA) of the Philippines requires the free and prior informed consent of indigenous peoples for projects that impact their ancestral lands. When the affected Ibaloi communities learned of the San Roque Dam project, they immediately raised their concerns about the adverse impacts of this project. A report released in 2001 by the Office of the Presidential Assistant on Indigenous Peoples' Affairs validated claims that project proponents did not obtain the free and prior informed consent of affected

Indigenous Peoples and the Human Rights-Based Approach to Development

indigenous communities and that consultations were conducted only after the project was already underway. Despite the violation of Philippine law and JBIC policies on indigenous people, and in spite of efforts by affected communities to reach out to the Philippine government, JBIC and the power company through dialogues, appeals and petition letters, the project was built and started commercial operations in May 2003. At present, there remain serious outstanding economic and social issues, which need to be addressed by project proponents and JBIC. These include the worsening siltation build-up in the upstream of the dam project, affecting the indigenous peoples in the area.

Kelau Dam, Malaysia (2005–)

The Kelau Dam was proposed to meet the water demands of Selangor State and Kuala Lumpur in Malaysia. The project plans to transfer around 1.5 billion litres of water per day from the Kelau River in Pahang State to the Langat River in Selangor State. JBIC approved the 82.04 billion yen loan to the Malaysian government for the Kelau dam on 31 March 2005.

The dam will have serious impacts on the Kelau River ecosystem and will require the resettlement of 325 Orang Asli (indigenous people) and 120 Malay farmers, thereby seriously affecting their lives and livelihoods. Yet there is no clear need for the water: studies by Malaysian NGOs show that the current water supply system in Selangor State is wasteful and beset with inefficiencies. Investment in water conservation measures and reduction in system losses could result in water savings that would make the construction of the Kelau Dam unnecessary.

Although the project proponents claim that the people are agreeable to the project, the Centre for Orang Asli Concerns (COAC) found that the affected Temuan families did not give their free, prior and informed consent to the relocation. According to the village chief,

> It's true I say I support (the project). Because we Orang Asli have been weakened. Others weaken us. They say resettle, we have to resettle. ... Officers come in and say, "Tok Batin, resettle" and we are forced to resettle. They pressure us until we cannot think anymore. If we have a choice, we want to stay where we are. The land is our ancestors' land. We have been there for a long time. But what can we do? The Government wants to give water to Selangor.[23]

Furthermore, the Government of Malaysia has reported to the JBIC that the Orang Asli houses of Sungai Temir will not be inundated and the people can choose either to stay or to move from the current village to a new settlement in Sungai Bilut. This decision, however, has not been conveyed to the Temuan families at all.[24]

Sakhalin II Oil Development Project, Russia

The Sakhalin II Project in Russia is developing oil and natural gas reserves that will be exported to Japan, Korea and other countries. The JBIC and the European Bank for

---

[23] Centre for Orang Asli Concerns (2002). The Orang Asli position in the proposed Kelau Dam Project. Report submitted to Friends of the Earth, Japan.

[24] Centre for Orang Asli Concerns. The letter submitted to JBIC on 17 and 28 March 2005.

Reconstruction and Development (EBRD) are now considering co-financing the project. The project could greatly damage the Indigenous Peoples of the North of Sakhalin Region as well as the fisheries and ecosystems in the Sea of Okhotsk.

The Sakhalin II Project started to cause many problems for indigenous peoples (including damage to fish resources) in 1998 when the Molikpaq platform was installed. In spite of this, the proponent, Sakhalin Energy, and its shareholders (Royal Dutch/Shell Group, Mitsui and Mitsubishi) did not pay an appropriate compensation directly to indigenous peoples' communities. Another concern is that the project will cause the reduction of fish stocks through the construction of a pipeline trench across the salmon spawning rivers. Reindeer pastures and the number of forest animals will also be cut down by the building of onshore pipelines that will pollute the environment. The harm done to the animal and plant world in traditional land-use areas takes a direct toll on the vital activities of indigenous peoples.

The Sakhalin indigenous peoples have demanded to conduct an Independent Ethnological Expert Review in order to estimate the past, current and future impact of the Sakhalin II Project on the environment and traditional use of natural resources of the Sakhalin indigenous peoples. This review should be different from the Environment, Social and Health Impact Assessment which was done by "Sakhalin Energy" with regard to indigenous peoples' issues. The people have submitted letters to JBIC on their concerns and demands since 2004.

Since the proponent requested funding for the project before October 2003 when the new JBIC Guidelines came into effect, JBIC applied its guidelines only partially to the project. JBIC established the "Environmental Forum on Sakhalin II" in order to ensure transparency and equity in its review process. Japanese fisher folk, experts and NGOs are concerned about the significant impacts of the project on Japan itself. Sessions of the environmental forum took place nine times from October 2004 till May 2005 in Tokyo and Sapporo. This forum for the specific programme was epoch-making under the new JBIC Guidelines.

It is still a question, however, how the forum will address the problems caused by the project. JBIC has failed to propose any concrete measures to address the issues raised by the participants in the forum. In addition, the agenda of the forum was limited to issues related to the impacts in Japan, while issues related to the Sakhalin indigenous peoples were excluded from the agenda.

V. Experiences and lessons learned using the JBIC Guidelines

Failure to properly assess social and environmental impacts prior to approval

JBIC's project appraisal process is seriously deficient and needs radical improvement. JBIC failed to adequately assess the projects' social and environmental impacts prior to project approvals. Instead, JBIC relied on information provided by the governments and/or the project developers. Such failure has resulted in impacts far beyond what was originally predicted, destroying the lives and livelihoods of many thousands of people. In particular, the assessment of social impacts on affected indigenous communities was minimal, if not under-estimated, such that it was not able to capture and bridge a better appreciation of the particularities of indigenous communities. Likewise, there is a tendency to measure social and cultural impacts in economic and material terms, while these concerns are more intergenerational. Indigenous communities commonly argue that these impacts cannot be mitigated by money or projects.

Failure to ensure proper consultation and release of information

JBIC and the project developers failed to release adequate information to affected communities and the public. In many cases, JBIC simply refused to release critical documents such as environmental impact assessments and resettlement plans, citing lack of government approval. While JBIC's new Environmental Guidelines mandate a higher standard of information disclosure than previously, JBIC is still refusing to release important documents for projects already funded or in the pipeline. Furthermore, steps have not been taken to ensure access to information by affected communities.

Additionally, JBIC has failed to involve affected communities in meaningful decision-making, with respect for the right of indigenous peoples to free, prior and informed consent. This has resulted in projects being implemented without the involvement or participation of affected communities. Too often, indigenous communities are offered funds and projects, instead of having a substantial and meaningful dialogue with the necessary and important information provided to affected communities. Likewise, functional structures of traditional leadership are not acknowledged or recognized. There have even been attempts to bribe local leaders to support and endorse the project.

Inadequate monitoring and evaluation during and after project construction

JBIC's monitoring and evaluation procedures are clearly inadequate. The modus operandi for JBIC in the past has been to disburse funds and then leave the project to the governments to implement. As a result, communities are left to suffer impacts, without any recourse or access to the project funders. In many cases, promises of compensation are not honoured by the government or implementing agency. Yet, JBIC refused to discuss these issues with the affected communities and directed the people to talk to the government instead. Since many of these projects would not have been pushed through without JBIC funding, JBIC has a responsibility to ensure that the projects are implemented in accordance with JBIC guidelines and international human rights standards.

In some cases, such as the San Roque Dam Project, JBIC did undertake regular monitoring missions as a result of pressure from affected communities and International NGOs. However, there was minimal follow-up to these missions and no means of ensuring that the JBIC recommendations were adhered to by project developers and the government.

No mechanism to deal with outstanding problems

Many projects have resulted in communities being worse off than they were before. Yet JBIC has no mechanism for dealing with the serious environmental and social problems created by its projects. There is a growing demand for JBIC to take responsibility for repairing the harm caused by its previously funded projects. JBIC should allocate resources for retroactive compensation, mitigation and rehabilitation measures.

VI. Recommendations for strategic engagement

JBIC stipulates in its review of Guidelines the following:

> JBIC verifies the status of the implementation of the Guidelines, and, based on its findings, conducts a comprehensive review of the Guidelines within five (5) years of their enforcement. Revisions may then be made as needed. When making revisions, JBIC will seek the opinions of the Japanese Government, the governments of developing countries, Japanese companies, experts, NGOs etc., while maintaining transparency in the process.[25]

Since the Guidelines came into effect on 1 October 2003, JBIC is set to conduct a comprehensive review and revision of the Guidelines by October 2008.

As demonstrated by the experiences of indigenous communities with JBIC-funded projects, and based on an analysis of the present guidelines and its use, there is an urgent need to engage with JBIC on policy reforms to include the following:

1. For JBIC to formulate a specific guideline for Indigenous Peoples such as that of the World Bank and the Asian Development Bank. This Policy formulation must take into account existing international laws and instruments pertaining to indigenous peoples such as the ILO 169, the right to Free, Prior and Informed Consent or "FPIC", among others. It should also take into account the "Rights-Based Approach to Development" as its over-all framework. Likewise, the policy formulation of JBIC on Indigenous Peoples must ensure the direct involvement of indigenous peoples and their active participation in the process in order to ensure that their views, concerns and issues are taken into account and integrated in the finalization of the Policy.

2. In the absence of a separate Policy on Indigenous Peoples, the present JBIC Guidelines must ensure the implementation of the right of indigenous peoples in relation to their land and resources. Likewise, the existing internationally-accepted right to FPIC must be operationalized in "accordance with the spirit of the relevant international declarations and treaties".

3. Environmental and social impact studies should fully account for the specificities of indigenous peoples, to include socio-cultural impacts, intergenerational livelihood activities and views of affected indigenous peoples on compensation or non-compensation of losses which are beyond material measurement. These studies must ensure a process of transparency and validation by affected communities, prior to consideration by JBIC for project funding.

4. To recommend accountability measures on the part of JBIC to address violations on its own Guidelines through the Objection Procedure. This shall include measures on just compensation of affected communities, mitigation and rehabilitation of damaged environments and sources of people's livelihood.

[25] Japan Bank for International Cooperation. *JBIC Guidelines for Confirmation of Environmental and Social Considerations*, p.12.

Indigenous Peoples and the Human Rights-Based Approach to Development

3

World Bank, International Finance Corporation and Indigenous Peoples in Asia

Fergus MacKay

I. Introduction

The International Bank for Reconstruction and Development ("the World Bank" or "the Bank") was established as an intergovernmental organization in 1944 with the primary mandate of financing reconstruction and facilitating economic development post World War II. This mandate has been reinterpreted a number of times over the years culminating with a professed focus on poverty alleviation today.[1] While not true for all of its activities, poverty alleviation has largely been equated with economic growth and heavily influenced by neo-liberal economic principles. This is particularly the case for the Bank's structural adjustment programmes and other non-project based interventions, such as technical assistance loans aimed at revising legislation and government policy.

As of May 2001, 184 countries were members of the Bank. By virtue of the Bank's Articles of Agreement, an international treaty that acts as the constitution of the organization, and as a precondition to membership in the Bank, these countries must also be members of the International Monetary Fund. The Articles of Agreement vests ultimate decision-making power in a Board of Governors and a Board of Executive Directors, including the authority to interpret the scope and meaning of the Articles.[2] There are presently 24 Executive Directors, five of which are appointed by the United States, Japan, Germany, France and the United Kingdom, being the countries holding the largest capital shares in the Bank, while the remainder are elected by the Governors representing the other 179 member states. Voting rights in the Bank are weighted according to the amount of capital shares held by each country. The United States by itself, as the largest donor, initially held over 37 percent of the voting power and today holds 16.50 percent.

A number of other institutions have been created and today form what is known as the World Bank Group ("the WBG"). These include the International Finance Corporation ("the IFC"), which was established in 1956 to provide financing for private sector entities working in developing countries rather than governments; the International Development Association, established in 1960 to provide grants to some governments rather than loans; and the Multilateral Investment Guarantee Agency ("MIGA"), which provides investment guarantees including political risk insurance to private sector bodies working in developing countries. The Bank is also a specialized agency of the United Nations by virtue of a 1948 Relationship Agreement with the UN Economic and Social Council. As such it is also a member of and active participant in the Inter-Agency Support Group to the UN Permanent Forum on Indigenous Issues and participates in other UN bodies, including the Working Group on Indigenous Populations.

---

[1] *Working for a World Free of Poverty*. World Bank: Washington DC, 2003. Available at: http://siteresources.worldbank.org/EXTABOUTUS/Resources/wbgroupbrochure.pdf

[2] International Bank for Reconstruction and Development, *Articles of Agreement*, art. 9 (describing the process of review for any question of interpretation of the provisions of the Agreement). See, also, J. Head, *For Richer or for Poorer: Assessing the Criticisms Directed at Multilateral Development Banks*, 52 U. Kan. L. Rev. 241, at 271 (2004) (stating that "the charters place with the MDBs' own governing bodies the complete authority to decide questions of charter interpretation or application"). For the views of two former General Counsels, see, Ibrahim F. I. Shihata, *Human Rights, Development, and International Financial Institutions*, 8 Am. U. J. Int'l L. & Pol'y 27, 29-30 (1992) and; K-Y. Tung, *Shaping Globalization*, supra note 43, at 34 (stating "It should be noted that while the General Counsel's opinions carry enormous weight, the ultimate authority in interpreting the Articles of Agreement rests with the Bank's Executive Directors, of whom there are twenty-four representing the 184 member countries").

The WBG is one of the largest financers of development projects and activities in the world. In 1999-2000, for instance, the Bank's cumulative lending alone was US$162,789 million. The WBG also styles itself as, and is perceived by some to be, the world's pre-eminent development institution. Therefore, in addition to the amount of funds lent or granted, it also wields substantial influence over other actors in terms of policies and ideas. This applies to both governments and private sector entities alike. With regard to governments, for instance, the Bank has supported the revision of mining and petroleum related laws and institutions in over 100 countries in the period 1990-2003.[3] These revisions almost always focus in liberalizing the sector and creating incentives for foreign investment, while at the same time often reducing the regulatory powers of the state. In the private sector, more than 29 of the world's largest commercial banks have adopted the IFC's policies on environmental and social issues and apply these to the projects they finance. Industry groups or specific companies also often reference and apply WBG standards to their activities and projects.

Given the global reach of its activities and its influence on other actors, it is not surprising that the WBG often affects indigenous peoples, both directly and indirectly. In some cases, indigenous peoples are affected by a specific project financed by the WBG, in others they are affected by programmatic lending, such as structural adjustment or technical assistance loans. Most attention has focused on project lending as it affects indigenous peoples while the impact of programmatic lending has not been sufficiently critiqued. This is a serious omission given that until recently World Bank programmatic lending comprised around one half of the total amount of financing provided by the Bank and has a much greater impact that specific projects.

This paper focuses on the impact of WBG activities on indigenous peoples with a particular focus on the policies adopted by the WBG to mitigate adverse impacts on indigenous peoples. Section II addresses the World Bank and its policies that deal directly with or affect indigenous peoples. Section III focuses on the IFC's draft policy on indigenous peoples. Section IV provides a brief overview of the nature and extent of indigenous peoples' engagement with the WBG. Finally, Section V identifies and discusses a number of issues concerning future strategic engagement.

II. The International Bank for Reconstruction and Development

Since the early 1980s, the World Bank Group has adopted a number of policies – referred to as safeguard policies – designed to mitigate harm to indigenous peoples in WBG-financed projects. In 1981, it published a study entitled *Economic Development and Tribal Peoples:*

---

[3] *Striking a Better Balance. The World Bank Group and Extractive Industries. The Final Report of the Extractive Industries Review*, Vol. I, December 2003 (hereinafter 'EIR Report'), 8. For a detailed overview of World Bank structural and sectoral lending related to extractive industries, see, H. Mainhardt-Gibbs, *The World Bank Extractive Industries Review: The Role of Structural Reform Programs towards Sustainable Development Outcomes*, August 2003. Available at: http://www.eireview.org/doc/Structural%20Adjustment%20EIR%20Exec%20Summary%20Mainhardt%20Aug%2014.doc

4

Human Ecologic Considerations, which sought to provide guidelines for Bank operations.[4] It states that the Bank should avoid "unnecessary or avoidable encroachment onto territories used or occupied by tribal groups;" ruled out involvement with projects not agreed to by indigenous peoples; required guarantees from borrowers that they would implement safeguard measures; and advocated respect for indigenous peoples' right to self-determination.[5]

The first formal policy followed a year later in 1982 and was called *Operational Manual Statement 2.34 Tribal People in Bank-Financed Projects*. Although OMS 2.34 was adopted in response to "internal and external condemnation of the disastrous experiences of indigenous groups in Bank-financed projects in the Amazon region,"[6] it failed to incorporate many of the protections proposed in the 1981 study. Moreover, an internal implementation review conducted in 1986-87 found that only two out of 33 Bank projects substantially complied with the policy.[7] Implementation failures and sustained criticism of Bank projects by indigenous peoples, NGOs and others,[8] led the Bank to revise and update OMS 2.34, concluding in 1991 with the adoption of Operational Directive 4.20 on Indigenous Peoples ("OD 4.20").[9]

OD 4.20 strengthened Bank policy on indigenous peoples by requiring indigenous peoples' informed participation; accounting for indigenous preferences in project design; strengthening domestic legislation on indigenous peoples' rights; paying special attention to securing indigenous land and resource rights; and developing specialized Indigenous Peoples' Development Plans to provide for culturally appropriate benefits and mitigation plans in all projects affecting indigenous peoples.[10] While OD 4.20 was an improvement over its predecessor, it did not assuage critics of Bank projects, especially since compliance with the policy was inconsistent at best.[11]

OD 4.20 was the subject of a protracted and contentious revision process and was replaced in May 2005 by Operational Policy 4.10 on Indigenous Peoples ("OP 4.10" or "the OP"). This new policy, which now only applies to the public sector arm of the WBG, is technically a

---

[4]   Robert Goodland, Economic Development and Tribal Peoples: Human Ecologic Considerations (World Bank 1982).

[5]   *Id.* at 3, 27.

[6]   B. Kingsbury, *Operational Policies of International Institutions as Part of the Law-Making Process: The World Bank and Indigenous Peoples, in*, The Reality of International Law: Essays in Honour of Ian Brownlie 324 (G.S. Goodwin-Gill & S. Talmon eds., Clarendon Press 1999).

[7]   *See* Office of Environmental and Scientific Affairs, World Bank, Tribal Peoples and Economic Development: A Five Year Implementation Review of OMS 2.34 (1982-1986) and a Tribal Peoples' Action Plan (World Bank 1987) (finding that projects were not complying with the new procedures for work involving tribal peoples).

[8]   *See generally Andrew Gray, Development Policy, Development Protest: The World Bank, Indigenous Peoples and NGOs,* in The Struggle for Accountability: The World Bank, NGOs, and Grassroots Movements 267 (Jonathan A. Fox & L. David Brown eds., 1998) (describing the Bank projects and policies affecting indigenous peoples and criticism thereof).

[9]   See Shelton Davis, *The World Bank and Operational Directive 4.20: The World Bank and Indigenous People, in* Indigenous Peoples and International Organisations 75 (Lydia van de Fliert ed., 1994) (discussing the revision process completed by the Bank to their policy on indigenous peoples and the contours of the new policy, OD 4.20).

[10] *Operational Directive 4.20 on Indigenous Peoples* (1991), *at* http://wbln0018.worldbank.org/Institutional/Manuals/OpManual.nsf/0/0F7D6F3F04DD70398525672C007D08ED?OpenDocument

[11] *See* Thomas Griffiths & Marcus Colchester, Report on a Workshop on 'Indigenous Peoples, Forests and the World Bank: Policies and Practice' 9-10 (2000) at http://www.bicusa.org/mdbs/wbg/FinalsynthesisOctober2000.pdf (noting substantial failures to comply with the policy).

conversion of OD 4.20 to a new policy format rather than a full-blown revision.[12] Drafting commenced in 1996[13] and a draft for discussion was released to the public in March 2001.[14] A number of other drafts were subsequently produced.[15] These drafts were repeatedly and vigorously repudiated by indigenous peoples for being inconsistent with their internationally guaranteed rights and for offering few meaningful guarantees in relation to Bank-financed projects.[16] The same was also the case for the final policy which was adopted on 10 May 2005. The IFC will continue to use OD 4.20 until it adopts its new standards in early 2006.

Indigenous peoples have consistently demanded that WBG safeguard policies must, at a minimum, provide for their right to free, prior and informed consent, recognition and protection of territorial rights, self-identification (as the fundamental criterion in determining the peoples covered by the policy), a prohibition of involuntary resettlement, and respect for indigenous peoples' right to self-determination.[17] They explain that in many cases they continue to experience severe negative impacts and human rights abuses in relation to WBG projects and therefore a strong and effective safeguard policy that is grounded in and consistent with international human rights law is needed. Negative impacts and abuses have also been identified in internal WBG performance evaluations,[18]

---

[12] The International Finance Corporation is presently adopting its own safeguard policies. *See infra* and International Finance Corporation, *Policy and Performance Standards on Social and Environmental Sustainability*, Public Release Draft September 22, 2005 (hereinafter "IFC Draft"), available at www.ifc.org/policyreview (esp., Performance Standard 7 on Indigenous Peoples and Performance Standard 5 on Involuntary Resettlement).

[13] *See* S. Davis et al., *Approach Paper on Revision of OD 4.20 on Indigenous Peoples at* http://wb1n0018.worldbank.org/essd/essd.nsf/28354584d9d97c29852567cc00780e2a/5e23e566bed37cd6852567cc0077f48d?OpenDocument (recommending certain revisions to OD 4.20, specifically to identification of indigenous peoples, policy objectives and framework, and measures and procedures to facilitate policy implementation).

[14] Draft OP 4.10, 23 March 2001, *at* http://lnweb18.worldbank.org/ESSD/sdvext.nsf/63ByDocName/PoliciesDraftOP410 March232001 For an extensive discussion of this draft, see Fergus MacKay, *Universal Rights or a Universe Unto Itself? Indigenous Peoples' Human Rights and the World Bank's Draft Operational Policy 4.10 on Indigenous Peoples*, 17 Am. U. Int'l L. Rev. 527 (2002).

[15] *See Draft Operational Policy 4.10 Indigenous Peoples, Revised Consultation Draft* (unpublished World Bank doc.), 17 May 2004. Available at: www.bicusa.org

[16] *Summary Report of World Bank Round Table Discussion of Indigenous Representatives and the World Bank on the Revision of the World Bank's Indigenous Peoples Policy, 18 October 2002*, at http://forestpeoples.gn.apc.org/Briefings/World%20Bank/wb_ip_round_table_summary_oct_02_eng.pdf See also, Thomas Griffiths, *Failure of Accountability: Indigenous Peoples, human rights and international development standards*. (Forest Peoples Programme, Moreton-in-Marsh 2003), at www.forestpeoples.org; *Summary of Consultations with External Stakeholders regarding the World Bank Draft Indigenous Peoples Policy (OP/BP 4.10) - last updated 7 October 2002 at* http://lnweb18.worldbank.org/ESSD/essd.nsf/1a8011b1ed265afd85256a4f00768797/c4a768e4f7c935f185256ba5006c75f3/$FILE/SumExtConsult-4-23-02.pdf; and, Indigenous Peoples Statement at the 19th Session of the UNWGIP (July 29, 2001) at: http://forestpeoples.gn.apc.org/briefings.htm (criticizing that draft OP 4.10: "does not build upon and reinforce the positive language in the existing policy; fails to incorporate many of the key recommendations made by indigenous peoples during previous consultations on the Bank's 'approach paper' on the revision process; uses language that confuses consultation with effective participation; lacks binding provisions that seek to guarantee indigenous land and resource security; fails to recognize the right to free, informed prior consent; does not prohibit the involuntary resettlement of indigenous peoples; is not consistent with existing and emerging international standards on human rights and sustainable development; and does not advance international standards for dealing with indigenous peoples in development").

[17] *Id.*

[18] See among others, *Implementation of Operational Directive 4.20 on Indigenous Peoples: An Evaluation of Results*. OED Report No. 25754, 10 April 2003, World Bank: Washington DC, at http://www-wds.worldbank.org/servlet/WDSContentServer/WDSP/IB/2003/05/01/000160016_20030501182633/additional/862317580_200306204005416.pdf; and, *Implementation of Operational Directive 4.20 on Indigenous Peoples: An independent desk review* January 10, 2003, Country Evaluation and Regional Relations (OEDCR), OED Report No. 25332, World Bank: Washington, D.C. 2003

and documented by NGOs and intergovernmental human rights bodies.[19] WBG studies also have recognized that indigenous peoples "have often been on the losing end of the development process."[20]

The United Nations Permanent Forum on Indigenous Issues, the body responsible for overall coordination of UN system activities relating to indigenous peoples, has echoed indigenous peoples demands by recommending in 2003 that the WBG continue to address issues currently outstanding, including Bank implementation of international customary laws and standards, in particular human rights instruments, full recognition of customary land and resource rights of indigenous peoples, recognition of the right of free, prior informed consent of indigenous peoples regarding development projects that affect them, and prohibition of the involuntary resettlement of indigenous peoples.[21]

Indigenous peoples also point to the WBG's own evaluations that demonstrate that it repeatedly fails to adhere to its own policy prescriptions on indigenous peoples and that for this reason compliance, enforcement and grievance mechanisms must be built into policies and incorporated into project instruments and loan agreements if safeguards are to be meaningful and effective. A 2003 WBG review of OD 4.20, for instance, found that it was only applied, fully or partially, in 50 percent of projects affecting indigenous peoples and of those only 14 percent had the required Indigenous Peoples Development Plan.[22] Another WBG evaluation found that

> Project results for [indigenous peoples] were not as satisfactory in the energy and mining, transportation, and environment sectors, which comprised 65 percent of Bank commitments evaluated for this second phase, and include projects with significant potential to harm IP. The majority of these projects neither mitigated adverse effects on IPs nor ensured that they received an equitable share of benefits;[23]

The evaluation also found that only 38 percent of a sample of WBG projects which did apply the policy satisfactorily mitigated adverse impacts and ensured benefits for indigenous peoples.[24]

4

---

[19] *See* for instance, *Report of the Special Rapporteur on the situation of human rights and fundamental freedoms of indigenous people, Mr. Rodolfo Stavenhagen, submitted pursuant to Commission resolution 2001/57*. UN Doc. E/CN.4/2002/97, at para. 56 (observing that "…resources are being extracted and/or developed by other interests (oil, mining, logging, fisheries, etc.) with little or no benefits for the indigenous communities that occupy the land. Whereas the World Bank has developed operational directives concerning its own activities in relation to these issues …and some national legislation specifically protects the interests of indigenous communities in this respect, in numerous instances the rights and needs of indigenous peoples are disregarded, making this one of the major human rights problems faced by them in recent decades"). See, also, Korina Horta, *Rhetoric and Reality: Human Rights and the World Bank*, 15 Harvard Human Rights J. 227 (2002).

[20] *The World Bank Participation Source Book*. (World Bank: Washington D.C. 1996), at 251.

[21] *Report of the Permanent Forum on Indigenous Issues on its Second Session*. UN Doc. E/2003/43; E/C.19/2003/22, at para. 33.

[22] OED Report No. 25332, *supra* note 18. For a discussion of institutional constraints in relation to safeguard policy compliance rates, see N. Bridgeman, *World Bank Reform in the "Post Policy" Era*, 13 Georgetown Int'l Enviro. L. Rev. 1013 (2001).

[23] OED Report No. 25754, *supra* note 18.

[24] *Id.*

WBG staff has responded to indigenous peoples' demands by stating that that such measures cannot be included in WBG policies at least in part because the WBG is prohibited from addressing the full range of human rights issues by its Articles of Agreement,[25] which requires that it not interfere in the "political affairs" of its members.[26] Indigenous peoples counter that in contemporary international law, human rights are not considered to be domestic political affairs, but are of international concern, and at any rate that, since 1991, OD 4.20 has had as its stated "broad objective" ensuring "that the development process fosters full respect for their dignity, human rights, and cultural uniqueness."[27]

A United Nations study concluded that if the WBG's position on human rights "were to be considered legitimate, it would seriously erode the international rule of law."[28] The views of the present General Counsel offer some encouragement that the WBG may review its position on human rights. In February 2004, he stated that the WBG "can and must take into account human rights violations in its process of making economic decisions. Moreover, because of the way international law has evolved with respect to concepts of sovereignty, and the range of issues that are considered to be of global concern, in doing so the Bank will not fall foul of the political prohibitions of the Articles."[29]

A. Operational Policy 4.10 on Indigenous Peoples of 10 May 2005

With this background in mind, this section summarizes and comments on selected provisions of OP 4.10 of 10 May 2005. The OP will likely be the standard applied by the public sector arm of the WBG for the next decade or more. Special attention is devoted to the use and meaning of the language 'free, prior and informed consultation resulting in broad community support' because in many respects the efficacy of the protections set forth in the OP may turn on its interpretation and use in practice.

1. The 'Preambular' Paragraphs

Paragraph 1 provides that OP 4.10 "contributes to the Bank's mission of poverty reduction and sustainable development by ensuring that the development process fully respects the dignity, human rights, economies and cultures of indigenous peoples." This statement can

---

[25] See The World Bank, International Bank for Reconstruction and Development, *Articles of Agreement*, (setting forth the purposes of the Bank), art. IV, sec.10 ("[t]he Bank and its officers shall not interfere in the political affairs of any member; nor shall they be influenced in their decisions by the political character of the member or members concerned"), at http://www.worldbank.org/html/extdr/backgrd/ibrd/arttoc.htm See, also, Ibrahim F.I. Shihata, Democracy and Development, 46 Int'l & Comp. L.Q. 635, 638 (1997); and Ibrahim F. I. Shihata, *Human Rights, Development, and International Financial Institutions*, 8 Am. U. J. Int'l L. & Pol'y 27, 28 (1992). For a contrary view, see, Sigrun I. Skogly, The Human Rights Obligations of the World Bank And the International Monetary Fund (2001); and M. Darrow, Between Light and Shadow. The World Bank, The International Monetary Fund and International Human Rights Law (2003).

[26] See Summary Report of World Bank Round Table Discussion of Indigenous Representatives and the World Bank on the Revision of the World Bank's Indigenous Peoples Policy, supra note 16.

[27] Supra note 10, at para. 6.

[28] Globalization and it full impact on human rights. Final report submitted by J. Oloka-Onyango and Deepika Udagama, in accordance with Sub-Commission decision 2000/105. UN Doc. E/CN.4/Sub.2/2003/14, at para. 37.

[29] R. Danino, *The Legal Aspects of the World Bank's Work on Human Rights*. Paper presented at the New York University/ Ethical Globalization Initiative Conference on Human Rights and Development: Towards Mutual Reinforcement, 1 March 2004, at 5. An edited version of this paper was published as: R. Danino: The Legal Aspects of the World Bank's Work on Human Rights: Some Preliminary Thoughts. In: Human Rights and Development Towards Mutual Reinforcement (P. Alston & M. Robinson eds., 2005).

4

be read two ways: as a conclusion – i.e., the OP as it presently stands does now ensure that the development process fully respects indigenous peoples' dignity, human rights, etc., or; as a forward looking statement requiring that interpretation and implementation of the OP should be consistent with indigenous peoples' dignity, human rights, etc. If it is the former, this is a dubious assertion as the OP itself clearly does not fully respect indigenous peoples' human rights, economies, and cultures. If it is the latter, the OP should be interpreted and applied so as to fully respect indigenous peoples' cultures, human rights, dignity and economies. This language is significantly different that OD 4.20, which states that fostering full respect for indigenous peoples' dignity, human rights, etc., is a broad objective of the OD itself.

Paragraph 1 also states that for all projects proposed for Bank financing that affect indigenous peoples, the borrower must engage in free, prior and informed consultation ("FPICon") with indigenous peoples.[30] It continues that the Bank "will provide project financing only where [FPICon] results in broad community support to the project by the affected Indigenous Peoples." The definition and application of FPICon and 'broad community support' are key issues requiring clarification in the OP and may in large part determine whether the OP can be an effective safeguard for indigenous peoples' rights and interests. FPICon and broad community support are addressed in detail below.

Paragraph 1 further provides that Bank-financed projects will include measures to avoid potential adverse effects or where avoidance is "not feasible" to "minimize, mitigate, or compensate for such effects." In relation to this, in the past the Bank has often determined feasibility in solely economic terms, i.e., avoidance is not possible because it makes the project infeasible by raising costs. Finally, paragraph 1 provides that Bank projects will be designed to "ensure that Indigenous Peoples receive social and economic benefits that are culturally appropriate and gender and inter-generationally inclusive." For many indigenous peoples, the term 'inter-generational' includes ancestors and future generations: if the Bank is to fully respect indigenous peoples' cultures, such relationships must also be respected. Most likely, however, the OP is referring to generations in the sense of youth, adults and elders.

Paragraph 2 explains that the Bank recognizes that indigenous peoples' cultures and identities are "inextricably" related to traditional lands and resources and, therefore, "different risks and impacts can be expected in development projects." It also acknowledges that indigenous peoples often have limited ability to assert and defend their rights and interests at the domestic level and to participate in and benefit from development. Finally, consistent with the Final Declaration of the 2002 World Summit on Sustainable Development, it affirms that indigenous peoples "play a vital role in sustainable development," and that their rights are receiving increased attention and recognition in domestic and international law.[31]

---

[30] Footnote 3 explains that the OP applies to all project components affecting indigenous peoples "regardless of the source of financing," presumably meaning that the OP applies when the Bank is a co-financer as well as the sole donor and irrespective of the particular source of financing within the Bank.

[31] *Report of the World Summit on Sustainable Development, Johannesburg, South Africa, 26 August-4 September 2002.* UN Doc. A/CONF.199/20/Corr.1, at 10, art. 25.

2. Self-identification/definition of indigenous peoples (Paras. 3 and 4)

The OP does not employ a specific definition of the term "indigenous peoples" as does OD 4.20. Instead, it states that there is "no universally accepted definition" and therefore, it will "not define the term."[32] Paragraph 4, however, states that for the purposes of the OP, the term "indigenous peoples" refers to "a distinct, vulnerable, social and cultural group" possessing a number of characteristics in varying degrees. These characteristics include: self-identification as indigenous and recognition by others; "collective attachment" to distinct habitats or territories and the natural resources therein; the presence of "customary cultural, social, economic or political institutions" separate from those of the dominant society; and, an indigenous language, often different from the national language.

Paragraph 4 further provides that indigenous peoples who have "lost collective" attachment because of "forced severance" remain eligible for application of the policy. Footnote 7 defines collective attachment to mean "that for generations there has been a physical presence in and economic ties to lands and territories traditionally owned, or customarily used or occupied by the group concerned, including areas which hold special significance for it, such as sacred sites. 'Collective attachment' also refers to the attachment of transhumant/nomadic groups to the territory they use on a seasonal or cyclical basis." Forced severance is defined as

> …loss of collective attachment to geographically distinct habitats or ancestral territories occurring within the concerned group members' lifetime because of conflict, government resettlement programs, dispossession from their lands, natural calamities or incorporation of such territories into an urban area. … "urban area" normally means a city or large town, and takes into account all of the following characteristics, no single one of which is definitive: (a) the legal definition of the area as urban under domestic law; (b) a high population density; and (c) a high proportion of non-agricultural economic activities relative to agricultural activities.

This definition of forced severance is highly problematic for a number of reasons. First, loss of collective attachment "within the concerned group members' lifetime" probably refers to a period of 50-80 years, and therefore would exclude loss of lands and resources predating this period, lands and resources with which indigenous peoples most likely continue to maintain a variety of relationships. Second, the definition of urban areas would exclude non-legally designated areas, smaller population centres or population centres with a high proportion of agricultural activities. *Colono* or migrant communities established on indigenous lands in the Amazon, for instance, would not qualify as urban areas under the policy and, assuming that such colonization did not occur outside of the lifetime of the members, unless this could be characterized as "dispossession from their lands," would not qualify as a forced severance.

Finally, paragraph 4 provides that determinations of whether indigenous peoples are affected by a Bank project, thereby triggering the application of the OP, "may require a technical judgment (see paragraph 8)." Paragraph 8 contains the screening procedures through which the Bank determines the presence of indigenous peoples in a project area.

---

[32] It does note, in para. 4, that indigenous peoples may be referred to in different countries as "'indigenous ethnic minorities,' 'aboriginals,' 'hill tribes,' 'national minorities,' 'scheduled tribes' or 'tribal groups.'"

In making this determination, the Bank will seek the opinions of "qualified social scientists with expertise on the social and cultural groups in the project area." The Bank will also consult with indigenous peoples and the borrower government on this issue and the Bank may choose to "follow the borrower's framework for identification of indigenous peoples during project screening when that framework is consistent with [the OP]." In other words, the Bank may choose to follow national law and policy related to the identification of indigenous peoples if it decides that that law and policy is consistent with the requirements of the OP. Self-identification is clearly not the primary or only criteria that the Bank will assess to determine the presence of indigenous peoples for the purposes of applying the policy and the potential use of national law definitions could be very problematic.

3. Use of country systems (Para. 5)

Draft paragraph 5 was not found in OD 4.20 and represents a radical departure from previous WBG practice. It may also represent a substantial weakening of the safeguard policy system and raises a number of questions about the continued applicability of the Bank's complaints mechanism, the Inspection Panel.[33] It reads:

> If the borrower has a system that recognizes and protects the rights of indigenous peoples and provides an acceptable basis for achieving the objectives of this policy, the Bank may rely on that system. In deciding whether the borrower's system is acceptable, the Bank assesses the system and identifies all relevant legal, policy and institutional aspects that need to be strengthened. Aspects thus identified must be strengthened by the borrower prior to the Bank's agreement to rely upon the system to achieve the objectives of this policy.

This approach will essentially permit a borrower, provided the Bank approves, to apply its national legislation in Bank-financed projects instead of the Bank's operational policies. Note particularly that, in order to be approved by the Bank, the borrower's legislation need only comply with the objectives of the OP rather than the substantive requirements; this may allow much weaker standards to be applied to a project. Concern about this approach is sharpened given the nature of preliminary Bank papers on using country systems.[34] A draft operational policy called *Piloting the Use of Borrower Environmental and Social Safeguard Policies, Procedures, and Practices in Bank-Supported Projects*, for example, states that

> The Bank considers a country's relevant safeguard systems to be equivalent to its own safeguards policy framework if they are designed to achieve the objectives and adhere to the operational principles set out in Table A1 [see explanation below]. In determining equivalence, the Bank may take account of agreed improvements in the borrower's systems that take place under the project concerned, including Bank-supported efforts to strengthen relevant institutional and human capacity, and incentives and methods for implementation. In addition, the Bank assesses whether country implementation practices, track record, and capacity going forward are acceptable.[35]

---

[33] The Inspection Panel is only authorized to review Bank compliance with its operational policies and is not permitted to assess national law standards. On the Inspection Panel in general, see Dana Clark, Jonathan Fox and Kay Treakle (eds), Demanding Accountability. Civil Society Claims and the World Bank Inspection Panel (2003).

[34] *See* for instance, *Issues in Using Country Systems in Bank Operations. Operations* Policy and Country Services, World Bank, 8 October 2004 available at http://siteresources.worldbank.org/PROJECTS/Resources/40940-1097257794915/UseCountrySystems-10-08-04.pdf

[35] *Id.* at 9-10.

Among others, this language appears to sanction projects based on country systems, even where these systems are not equivalent to the Bank's safeguard framework provided the borrower agrees to make improvements as part of the project itself. This is worrying because borrowers have previously implemented projects without implementing agreed upon and concomitant safeguard measures, sometimes with the acquiescence of WBG managers, when these safeguards were mandatory prior conditions of project financing.[36]

With regard to indigenous peoples and determining country system/OP equivalency, Table 1A states that the policy objective is: "To design and implement projects in such a way that indigenous peoples (a) do not suffer adverse effects during the development process and (b) receive culturally compatible social and economic benefits."[37] The operational principles are:

1. Screen early for potential impacts on indigenous peoples, who are identified through criteria that reflect their social and cultural distinctiveness (including indigenous language, self-identification and identification by others, presence of customary institutions, or collective attachment to land).

2. Undertake meaningful consultation with affected indigenous peoples to solicit informed participation in designing and implementing measures to (a) avoid adverse impacts, or (b) when avoidance is not feasible, minimize, mitigate, or compensate for such effects.

3. Provide social and economic benefits to indigenous peoples in ways that are culturally appropriate, and gender and generationally inclusive. Consider options preferred by the affected groups.

4. Prepare mitigation plans, including documentation of the consultation process, and disclose them before appraisal in an accessible place and in a form and language that are understandable to key stakeholders.[38]

These statements clearly contradict what is found in the OP – note in particular the absence of FPICon resulting in broad community support – although it should be stressed that a footnote explains that these principles will be "updated as necessary when the ongoing conversion of the parent policy [OP 4.10] is completed."[39]

4. Project preparation

Paragraph 6 lists a number of requirements for projects proposed for Bank financing that may affect indigenous peoples. These requirements are:

■ Screening to determine if indigenous peoples have a collective attachment to the project area;

■ A social assessment conducted by the borrower;

---

[36] *See inter alia,* See Inspection Panel (2000) *The Quinghai Project: a component of the China-Western Poverty Reduction Project (Credit No.3255-CHA and Loan No.4501-CHA)* Inspection Panel Investigation Report, April 28, 2000; and, Dana Clark, *The World Bank and Human Rights: The Need for Greater Accountability.* 15 Harvard Human Rights Journal 205 (2002).

[37] *Supra* note 34, at 31.

[38] *Id.*

[39] *Id.*

■ A process of free, prior and informed consultation with indigenous peoples "at each stage of the project" to identify their views and to ascertain whether there is broad community support for the project;

■ Preparation of either an Indigenous Peoples Plan or an Indigenous Peoples Planning Framework; and

■ Disclosure of the IPP or IPPF.

Paragraph 7 adds that the level of detail needed to meet the requirements in paragraph 6 will be "proportionate" to the complexity of the project and "commensurate" with the nature and scale of the "potential effects" on indigenous peoples, whether positive or negative. This paragraph provides some degree of latitude to the Bank and borrower when examining the extent to which paragraph 6's requirements must be accounted for and implemented, and heightens the importance of adequate and participatory impact assessments. It should also be noted that there is no requirement that indigenous peoples participate in the impact assessments under the OP. If assessments are substandard or omit important elements or details, the Bank may choose a minimal application of the requirements in paragraph 6 and this is cause for concern given prior findings that potential impacts on indigenous peoples have often been underestimated, mischaracterized or unforeseen at the time of project preparation.[40]

5. Free, prior and informed consultation resulting in broad community support

a. Background

Indigenous peoples have consistently demanded that WBG policies on indigenous peoples recognize and require respect for indigenous peoples' right to give or withhold their free, prior and informed consent ("FPIC").[41] This was also recommended to the WBG by the World Commission on Dams ("WCD")[42] and, in 2004, by the Extractive Industries Review ("EIR").[43]

---

[40] Inter alia, supra note 18.

[41] See inter alia, Statement by indigenous peoples participating in the 19th Session of the UN Working Group on Indigenous Populations supra note 16. For an overview of treaty provisions, jurisprudence and development policies on indigenous peoples' right to FPIC, see Preliminary working paper on the principle of free, prior and informed consent of indigenous peoples in relation to development affecting their lands and natural resources that would serve as a framework for the drafting of a legal commentary by the Working Group on this concept submitted by Antoanella-Iulia Motoc and the Tebtebba Foundation. UN Doc. E/CN.4/Sub.2/AC.4/2004/4, (8 July 2004). See also, Fergus MacKay, Indigenous Peoples' Right to Free, Prior and Informed Consent and the World Bank's Extractive Industries Review, IV(2) Sustainable Dev. Law & Policy 43 (2004).

[42] Dams and Development: A new framework for decision-making. The Report of the World Commission on Dams (2000), 112 (see also, 267, 271, 278).

[43] Striking a Better Balance. The World Bank Group and Extractive Industries. The Final Report of the Extractive Industries Review (hereinafter "EIR Report"), Vol. I, December 2003, p. 21, 50, 60. The EIR was commissioned in 2001 by the President of the WBG, James Wolfensohn, to examine what role, if any, the WBG has in the oil, gas and mining sectors. It comprised a two year-long process of regional 'stakeholder' meetings, project site visits, commissioned research on particular issues, consideration of two internal WBG evaluations relating to extractive industries, and dialogue with World Bank staff. See Extractive Industries and Sustainable Development. An Evaluation of World Bank Group Experience. OED/OEG/OEU, World Bank (2003) and; Extracting Sustainable Advantage? A review of how sustainability issues have been dealt with in recent IFC & MIGA extractive industries projects. Final Report. Compliance Advisor Ombudsman, World Bank, April (2003). The EIR's Final Report, presented to the WBG in January 2004, was authored by Dr. Salim and contains a number of potentially far reaching recommendations about how the WBG conducts business and how human rights, including indigenous peoples' rights and FPIC, should be accounted for and respected in WBG policies and operations.

The WBG rejected recognition of and respect for FPIC in relation to the recommendations of the WCD and the EIR and has failed to incorporate it into OP 4.10 and the IFC's draft Performance Standards.[44] Instead, the WBG Board of Executive Directors approved, in its decision on the EIR made in August/September 2004, that the standard to be adopted and applied will be 'FPICon resulting in broad community support'.[45]

Of the 24 Executive Directors, only a few supported full recognition of and respect for FPIC. The Executive Director for Thailand/Indonesia, for instance, stated that "we do emphasise the community directly affected here as the principal stakeholder that should be recognized as the body for application of the notion of free, prior, informed consent (FPIC)." [46] The German and Swiss Executive Directors made similar statements,[47] while the Dutch Executive Director observed that

> we note a degree of ambiguity with regard to the internationally recognized rights of indigenous peoples. …It would be a major step forward if the Bank would address these aspects in a still more forthcoming and creative manner; much of what now still seems a controversy would become a new way of reconciling local tradition and the kind of globalisation that instils universally accepted principles of justice and participation in the operations of global players, be they industries, Banks or international organisations. It would therefore be a better understood signal if the approach of "prior informed consultation" would be replaced by the recognition of a necessary process of "consensus building" in line with the "broad support" by affected communities, including indigenous peoples that is already accepted as a prerequisite.[48]

b. What does the OP say?

As noted above, paragraph 1 of OP 4.10 provides that for all projects proposed for Bank-financing that affect indigenous peoples the borrower must engage in FPICon with indigenous peoples. FPICon is defined in footnote 4 as:

> "Free, prior and informed consultation with the affected Indigenous Peoples' communities" refers to a culturally-appropriate and collective decision-making process subsequent to meaningful and good faith consultation and informed participation regarding the preparation and implementation of the project. It does not constitute a veto right for individuals or groups (see paragraph 10).

---

[44] IFC Draft *supra* note 12.

[45] *Striking a Better Balance – The World Bank Group and Extractive Industries: The Final Report of the Extractive Industries Review. World Bank Group Management Response*, 17 September 2004, p. 7, 9, available at http://www.worldbank.org/ogmc

[46] *Statement of Rapee Asumpinpong, Extractive Industries Review and Management Response*, EDS2004-0626 (unpublished World Bank doc.), 2 August 2004, at 3.

[47] *Statement by Eckhard Deutscher, Striking a Better Balance – The World Bank Group and Extractive Industries: The Final Report of the Extractive Industries Review – Draft World Bank Group Management Response*, EDS2004-0612 (unpublished World Bank doc.), 2 August 2004, 3; and *Statement by Pietro Veglio, The World Bank Group and Extractive Industries: The Final Report of the Extractive Industries Review*, EDS2004-0610 (unpublished World Bank doc.), 2 August 2004, 4.

[48] *Statement by Ad Melkert, Management Response to the Extractive Industries Review*, EDS2004-0609 (unpublished World Bank doc.), 2 August 2004, at 3.

According to this definition, the following elements may be identified: meaningful and good faith consultation; informed participation; followed by a culturally appropriate and collective decision making process. Based on this definition, it appears that FPICon refers to a *process* comprised of the preceding elements rather than just consultation as such (see, however, the discussion on paragraph 10 below). Paragraph 1 continues that the Bank "will provide project financing only where [FPICon] results in broad community support to the project by the affected Indigenous Peoples." Conversely, if there is no 'broad community support' for the project, the Bank presumably will not continue to process or finance the project. This is ostensibly confirmed in paragraph 11, which states in part that:

> *The Bank subsequently satisfies itself through a review of the process and outcome of the consultation carried out by the borrower that the affected indigenous peoples' communities have provided their broad support to the project. The Bank pays particular attention to the social assessment and to the record and outcome of the free, prior and informed consultation with the affected Indigenous Peoples' communities as a basis for ascertaining whether there is such support. The Bank will not proceed further with project processing if it is unable to ascertain that such support exists.*

Note that the Bank "pays particular attention" to the social assessment in addition to the outcome of the FPICon process and therefore, indigenous peoples' support is not necessarily the decisive factor in whether the Bank may fund a project. In principle, this same language also does not preclude the Bank from assessing sources of information not mentioned above as a basis for ascertaining broad community support.

That FPICon resulting in broad community support is required in Bank projects is further confirmed in paragraph 6(c), which states that all proposed Bank projects that affect indigenous peoples require "a process of [FPICon] with the affected Indigenous Peoples' Communities at each stage of the project, and particularly during project preparation in order to fully identify their views and to ascertain their broad community support to the project (see paragraphs 10 and 11)." This section adds an important requirement: that FPICon and broad community support are required at each stage of the project. However, in this respect, it is unclear in the OP if broad community support is required for the development of the Indigenous Peoples Plan, clearly a stage of the project, – "in consultation with the affected Indigenous Peoples' Communities…" (para. 12 and Annex B) – and it does not appear to be required in relation to the Indigenous Planning Framework required in paragraph 13. This seems to be confirmed in paragraph 15 on disclosure (see below).

While FPICon is defined in a footnote in paragraph 1 (subject to paragraph 10), there is no definition of broad community support other than by reference to paragraph 11. What do these paragraphs say and do they help further explain these concepts? Paragraph 10 provides that where the project affects indigenous peoples – determined on the basis of Bank screening processes, in which indigenous peoples will be consulted, and the social assessment – the borrower shall engage in FPICon with them. "To ensure such consultation, the borrower:

(a) establishes an appropriate gender and inter-generationally inclusive framework that provides opportunities for consultation at each stage of project preparation and implementation among the borrower, the affected Indigenous Peoples' communities, the Indigenous Peoples Organizations (IPOs), if any, and other civil Society Organizations (CSOs) identified by the affected Indigenous Peoples' communities;

(b) use consultation methods[ ] appropriate to the social and cultural values of the affected Indigenous Peoples' communities and their local conditions and, in designing these methods, gives special attention to the concerns of Indigenous women, youth and children and their access to development opportunities and benefits; and

(c) provides the affected Indigenous Peoples' communities with all relevant information about the project (including an assessment of the potential adverse affects of the project on the affected Indigenous Peoples' communities) in a culturally appropriate manner at each stage of project preparation and implementation."

The footnote associated with the term 'consultation methods' in sub-paragraph (b) states that "Such consultation methods (including using indigenous languages, allowing time for consensus building, and selecting appropriate venues) facilitate the articulation by Indigenous Peoples of their views and preferences. The 'Indigenous Peoples' Guidebook (forthcoming) will provide good practice guidance on this and other matters."[49]

4

What is conspicuously absent from paragraph 10, however, is the informed participation component found in the footnoted definition of FPICon in paragraph 1. This omission is even more glaring given that ensuring informed participation is required in OD 4.20 and the Bank has repeatedly stated that OP 4.10 must, at a minimum, be consistent with OD 4.20. Informed participation is a substantially higher standard than consultation and requires active involvement in decision-making. Without explicit mention in paragraph 10 there is a real possibility that Bank staff and the borrower will mechanically follow the requirements set forth in paragraph 10, which require nothing more than consultation using methods designed by the borrower.

Paragraph 11, partly quoted above, provides that

In deciding whether to proceed with the project, the borrower ascertains, based on the social assessment (see paragraph 9) and the free, prior and informed consultation (see paragraph 10) whether the affected Indigenous Peoples' communities provide their broad support to the project. Where there is such support, the borrower prepares a detailed report that documents:

(a) the findings of the social assessment;

(b) the process of free, prior and informed consultation with the affected Indigenous Peoples' communities;

---

[49] According to the World Bank website: "A guidebook for Bank staff in implementing the Bank's Indigenous Peoples Policy is under preparation. Sections will be dedicated to special issues arising in each of the Bank's operational regions as well as the major sectors where projects affecting Indigenous Peoples can also be found. Specific guidelines for Bank staff in implementing the policy at different stages of the project cycle will also be provided," available at http://lnweb18.worldbank.org/ESSD/sdvext.nsf/63ByDocName/TheIndigenousPeoplesPolicyGuidebook

(c) additional measures, including project design modification, that may be required to address adverse effects on Indigenous Peoples and to provide them with culturally appropriate project benefits;

(d) recommendations for free, prior and informed consultations with and participation by Indigenous Peoples' communities during project implementation, monitoring and evaluation; and

(e) any formal agreements reached with Indigenous Peoples' communities and/or IPOs.

As discussed above, the Bank reviews this report and the social assessment (and possibly other sources) to determine if broad community support exists; if it does not exist, according to paragraph 11, the Bank will not continue with project processing. There are a number of important questions and issues raised by this paragraph.

i) There is no adequate definition of or attempt to explain what is meant by broad community support (i.e., does it mean a simple majority? three-quarters of the population? does it include decisions made in accordance with indigenous peoples' customary laws and through traditional or other representative institutions, etc.). The only indication of how to interpret the term is found in Bank Procedures 4.10, a policy to Bank staff adopted a month after OP 4.10, which states that Bank staff shall "verify that the borrower has gained the broad support from representatives of major sections of the community required under the policy;"[50]

ii) At this stage of project processing it is only the borrower and the Bank that ascertain whether broad community support exists – there is no explicit mechanism for indigenous peoples to state their views about the existence or non-existence of broad community support or the veracity of the borrower's report and there is no provision for independent verification of its existence or non-existence. This could and should be addressed by requiring formal agreements with indigenous peoples, as proposed in sub-paragraph (e), and by requiring that these agreements codify the terms and conditions of broad community support as well as the nature of subsequent FPICon processes. Ideally, these agreements should be reflected in loan covenants that provide indigenous peoples' standing to challenge future project implement should conditions be disregarded;

iii) In connection with point (ii) above, paragraph 15 provides for disclosure of the social assessment and draft Indigenous Peoples Plan/Indigenous Peoples Planning Framework to affected indigenous peoples' communities "in an appropriate form, manner and language." These are then approved by the Bank as the basis for project appraisal (the last phase of project processing prior to submission to the Board for approval) and subsequently released to the public and again to the affected indigenous peoples' communities. While indigenous peoples can raise issues of concern regarding the social assessment and draft IPP/IPPF with both the borrower and the Bank informally, there is no explicit mechanism to do so in the policy and it does not appear from this paragraph that broad community support

[50] *Bank Procedures 4.10 on Indigenous Peoples*, July 2005, at para. 7, available at: http://wbln0018.worldbank.org/Institutional/Manuals/OpManual.nsf/0/DBB9575225027E678525703100541C7D?OpenDocument

is required for the IPP/IPPF. The IPP/IPPF will in large part determine how the project will be implemented in relation to indigenous peoples and is therefore a critical component of the decision making process on whether to support the project;

iv) The elements of the social assessment, which are set forth in Annex A to OP 4.10, only indirectly concern assessing broad community support and then only implicitly as part of FPICon processes about avoiding or mitigating adverse impacts and benefits (see, paras. 2(d) and (e)). Therefore, it may be difficult to ascertain on the basis of a social assessment if broad community support exists. Further, while social impact assessments may be used as supplementary materials, the decisive voice in determining whether support exists must be indigenous peoples alone not the views of Bank or the borrower's consultants that conduct social impact assessments;

v) The borrower alone, subject to review by the Bank and the recommendations of a social assessment consultant, makes recommendations with regard to future FPICon and participation in the various project phases – it is unclear whether indigenous peoples will have a role in formulating these recommendations via the initial FPICon leading to broad community support or otherwise, and there is no guarantee that the borrower will not ignore or reformulate indigenous peoples' proposals in its report to the Bank. There is also no requirement that the borrower's report be disclosed to indigenous peoples;

vi) It is unclear what happens when broad community support has been obtained initially and the project has been approved and funds disbursed, but indigenous peoples withhold such support in later stages of the project (see, para. 6(c) requiring [FPICon] at each stage of the project to ascertain their broad community support);

vii) There is no built-in grievance/complaints/mediation mechanism for addressing disputes about the existence of broad community support in the initial project discussions. Provision is made in Annex B, paragraph 2(h), pertaining to the Indigenous Peoples Plan, "as needed," for "Accessible procedures appropriate to the project to address grievances by the affected Indigenous Peoples' communities arising from project implementation. When designing the grievance procedures, the borrower takes into account the availability of judicial recourse and customary dispute settlement mechanisms among the Indigenous Peoples." The IPP, however, is developed after broad community support is obtained and therefore any grievance mechanisms will only apply to project implementation rather than to the initial broad community support determination.

6. Lands and resources

As with FPIC, the requirement that broad community support be obtained is triggered by an actual or potential impact on indigenous peoples' traditional lands, territories and resources and therefore is dependent on a clear identification, recognition and protection of indigenous peoples' rights to lands, territories and resources traditionally owned or otherwise occupied and used. While this may seem an obvious point, it is not uncommon for states to limit FPIC to lands that are legally recognized in their own legal systems rather than the lands and territories traditionally owned by indigenous peoples in accordance with

4

their customary law and values, the standard employed in international law.[51] In many cases, there is a large disparity between the two categories and requiring FPIC only in connection with the former potentially exempts large areas of indigenous lands from the FPIC requirement.

In Guyana, for instance, FPIC applies only to "recognized" or titled lands thereby excluding approximately three-quarters of the lands traditionally owned and presently claimed by indigenous peoples.[52] The same also applies in the case of Australia's Northern Territory where FPIC applies to aboriginal lands recognized under the Aboriginal Land Rights (Northern Territory) Act 1976, but not to lands that may be owned pursuant to the 1993 Native Title Act (Cth). With regard to the latter, a 'right to negotiate', subject to arbitration if agreement cannot be reached, applies, not FPIC.[53] How does the OP define indigenous lands and territories for the purposes of determining if indigenous peoples are affected and, if so, requiring that FPICon resulting in broad community support applies and does it require recognition and regularization of rights to lands, territories and resources?

In September 2004, the WBG recognized that "indigenous peoples can be particularly vulnerable to projects that affect them due to their unique collective ties to lands, territories and natural resources."[54] At the same time it made a commitment that OP 4.10 will require recognition of the rights of indigenous peoples to lands and territories traditionally owned and customarily used and ensure that indigenous peoples receive due process guarantees, benefits and compensation "at least equivalent to what any landowner would be entitled to in the case of commercial development on their land…"[55] It is doubtful that draft OP 4.10 does adequately address land and resource rights and meets this commitment.

a. Identifying indigenous lands, territories and resources

According to paragraphs 6(c), 8, 9 and 10, indigenous peoples must be present in or have a collective attachment to the project area **and** be affected by the project for the FPICon resulting in broad community support requirement to become operative. Footnote 7 of OP 4.10 states that collective attachment, "means that for generations there has been a physical presence in and economic ties to lands and territories traditionally owned, or customarily used or occupied by the group concerned, including areas which hold special significance for it, such as sacred sites."

---

[51] See inter alia, The Mayagna (Sumo) Awas Tingni Community Case, Judgment of August 31, 2001. Inter-American Court of Human Rights, Series C No. 79, para. 146, 148, 164 (holding that states "must adopt the legislative, administrative, and any other measures required to create an effective mechanism for delimitation, demarcation, and titling of the property of indigenous communities, in accordance with their customary law, values, customs and mores"). Id. at 164, 173.

[52] See Government's Policy for Exploration and Development of Minerals and Petroleum of Guyana. Georgetown: Government of Guyana, (1997), at 12 ("Government has decided that recognized Amerindian lands would stand exempted from any survey, prospecting or mineral agreements unless the agreement of the Captain and Council for the proposal is obtained by the Guyana Geology and Mines Commission in writing").

[53] Native Title Act (Cth) 1993, sec. 25-44. The right to negotiate was substantially limited by the Native Title Amendment Act (Cth) 1998, which exempted entire categories of lands from the right to negotiate and, in some situations, authorized States and Territories to substitute reduced procedural rights. See G Nettheim, The Search for Certainty and the Native Title Amendment Act 1998 (Cth)", 22 U. of New South Wales L. J. 564 (1999).

[54] Supra note 45, at 8.

[55] Id. at 9

Apart from failing to recognize the substantial overlap between 'traditionally owned' and 'customarily used or occupied' in the sense that both are essentially grounded in and shaped by indigenous peoples' customary law, the above definition may not fully acknowledge indigenous peoples' multiple forms of attachments/relationships to traditional lands, territories and resources and reduces spiritual and religious relationships largely to site specific attachments. Also, OP 4.10 (para. 4) recognizes that some indigenous peoples may have lost collective attachment to all or parts of their traditional territories because of 'forced severance'. The problematic nature of the definition of forced severance is discussed above particularly in relation to its potential to artificially limit the application of the OP including the FPICon resulting in broad community support requirement.

b. Special considerations

Paragraph 16 states that due to indigenous peoples' close ties to lands and natural resources, special considerations apply which require that the borrower "pays particular attention" to the following when conducting social assessments and preparing IPPs/IPPFs:

- Customary rights, both individual and collective, pertaining to traditionally owned lands or territories, lands and territories customarily used or occupied and where access to natural resources is "vital to the sustainability of their cultures and livelihoods;"

- Protection of the above mentioned lands and resources from illegal – presumably 'illegal' under domestic law – encroachment or intrusion;

- The cultural and spiritual values that indigenous peoples attribute to their lands and resources;

- Indigenous peoples' natural resource management practices and the long-term sustainability of those practices.

Footnote 16 defines 'customary rights' to lands and resources as "patterns of long-standing community land and resource usage in accordance with indigenous peoples' customary laws, values, customs and traditions, including seasonal or cyclical use rather than formal legal title to land and resources issued by the State." The terminology used in paragraphs 16 (and 17) is confusing, although it is not clear how important this may be in practice. Specifically, the terms 'traditionally owned' and "customarily occupied or used" are largely synonymous – the only exception being in rare instances where indigenous peoples do not assign ownership or other rights under their customary laws. The real distinction is between lands owned in accordance with indigenous peoples' own laws and customs, but not legally recognized by the state, and those lands over which indigenous peoples hold title issued by the state that may or may not correspond to the full extent of lands, territories and resources traditionally/customarily owned.

Finally, mention is required of the phrase 'vital to sustainability of their cultures and livelihoods'. Non-indigenous people's property rights, including protection thereof, are not limited to those "vital" to cultural or livelihood sustainability and it is manifestly discriminatory to apply this standard to indigenous peoples.

c. Action on lands, territories and resources

Paragraph 17 of the OP provides:

4

4

If the project involves (a) activities that are contingent on establishing legally recognized rights to lands and territories that indigenous peoples traditionally occupied, or customarily used and occupied (such as land titling projects); or (b) the acquisition of such lands, the [Indigenous Peoples Plan] sets forth an action plan for the legal recognition of such occupation, or usage. Normally, the action plan is undertaken prior to project implementation; in some cases, however, the action plan may need to be carried out concurrently with the project itself. Such legal recognition may take the form of:

(a) full legal recognition of existing customary land tenure systems of Indigenous Peoples; or

(b) conversion of customary usage rights to communal and/or individual ownership rights.

If neither option is possible under domestic law, the IPP includes measures for legal recognition of perpetual or long term, renewable custodial or use rights.

Whether this language requires prior recognition of indigenous peoples' rights of ownership to lands, territories and resources turns on whether a project can be classified as (a) or (b) in the first paragraph and whether there is a procedure under domestic law that allows for such recognition. For instance, if a project does not contain activities contingent on establishing legally recognized rights – other than a mention of land titling projects, there is no indication as to what kind of projects will fall into this category – or the "acquisition" of such lands – 'acquisition' essentially means a taking or expropriation of indigenous lands for project-related purposes – paragraph 17 will not apply at all. It is also unclear why the Bank cannot require that domestic laws be adopted to recognize ownership rights if they do not exist, rather than requiring that the IPP provide for legal recognition of custodial or use rights; presumably the latter will require some form of legislative action anyway.

There is therefore not a clear statement in the OP that prior resolution of and adequate guarantees for indigenous peoples' rights to lands, territories and resources are required in relation to all projects that affect indigenous peoples' lands, territories and resources as promised by the Board. Additionally, conversion of customary rights to individual ownership rights without the express free, prior and informed consent of the affected indigenous peoples is contrary to human rights law and indigenous peoples' cultures and customs.[56]

d. Commercial exploitation of natural resources

If a project involves commercial exploitation of natural resources – defined in the OP as "minerals, hydrocarbon resources, forests, water, and hunting/fishing grounds – in indigenous peoples' territories (really areas where there is 'collective attachment'), paragraph

---

[56] See among others, *Report of the Committee set up to examine the representation alleging non-observance by Peru of the Indigenous and Tribal Peoples Convention, 1989 (No. 169), made under article 24 of the ILO Constitution by the General Confederation of Workers of Peru (CGTP)*. Doc. GB 270/16/4; GB 270/14/4 (1998), at para. 26 (finding that "when communally owned indigenous lands are divided and assigned to individuals or third parties, the exercise of their rights by indigenous communities tends to be weakened and generally end up losing all or most of the lands, resulting in a general reduction of the resources that are available to indigenous peoples when they keep their lands in common").

18 requires that "the borrower ensures that as part of the [FPICon] process the affected communities are informed of (a) their rights to such resources under statutory and customary law; (b) the scope and nature of such proposed commercial development and the parties involved or interested in such development; and (c) the potential effects of such development on their livelihoods, environments, and use of such resources." Also, the IPP must "enable" equitable benefit sharing and; at a minimum, the IPP must provide that indigenous peoples receive benefits in a culturally appropriate manner and that the "benefits, compensation and rights to due process [are] at least equivalent to that which any landowner with full legal title to the land would be entitled to in the case of commercial development on their land."

The appropriateness of this paragraph is entirely dependent on the definition of broad community support and whether this is implicitly required as part of the definition of FPICon. Rather than rely on this, it is critically important that this paragraph explicitly require that FPICon resulting in broad community support is required, particularly in light of the often severe and negative impact of extractive industry projects on indigenous peoples.[57] As stated by Victoria Tauli-Corpuz, an indigenous leader from the Philippines, "For many indigenous peoples throughout the world, oil, gas and coal industries conjure images of displaced peoples, despoiled lands, and depleted resources. This explains the unwavering resistance of most indigenous communities with any project related to extractive industries."[58] These abuses have also been documented by the WBG.[59]

e. Commercial exploitation of cultural resources or knowledge

Paragraph 19 concerns commercial exploitation of indigenous peoples' cultural resources or knowledge – the term "cultural resources" is not defined in the OP. Commercial exploitation is dependent on indigenous peoples' "prior agreement" and the IPP must reflect the nature and content of such agreements as well as provide for culturally appropriate and equitable benefit sharing. This formulation would be appropriate to use in connection with commercial exploitation of natural resources in paragraph 18 – or indeed in place of FPICon resulting in broad community support throughout the OP – and it is disappointing that this is not applied in that context as well.

f. Physical relocation and involuntary restrictions on access to protected areas

Paragraphs 20 and 21 concern physical relocation and involuntary restrictions on access to

---

[57] See inter alia, T. Downing, *Indigenous Peoples and Mining Encounters: Strategies and Tactics*, Minerals Mining and Sustainable Development Project: International Institute for Environment and Development and World Business Council: London (2002). (concluding that indigenous peoples experiences with the mining industry have largely resulted in a loss of sovereignty for traditional landholders; the creation of new forms of poverty due to a failure to avoid or mitigate impoverishment risks that accompany mining development; a loss of land; short and long-term health risks; loss of access to common resources; homelessness; loss of income; social disarticulation; food insecurity; loss of civil and human rights; and spiritual uncertainty). *Id.* at 3. See also, *Indigenous people and their relationship to land. Final working paper prepared by Mrs. Erica-Irene A. Daes, Special Rapporteur*. UN Doc. E/CN.4/Sub.2/2001/21. at paras. 66-7.

[58] Extracting Promises: Indigenous Peoples, Extractive Industries and the World Bank. (E. Caruso *et al.*, eds., Tebtebba Foundation & Forest Peoples Programme: Capitol Publishing House: Manilla, 2003), at 9.

[59] See OED Report No. 25754, *supra* note 18, at 26 (observing that mining and energy projects "risk and endanger the lives, assets, and livelihoods of [indigenous peoples]. Moreover, modern technology allows interventions in hitherto remote areas, causing significant displacement and irreparable damage to IP land and assets. In this context, IP living on these remote and resource rich lands are particularly vulnerable, because of their weaker bargaining capacity, and because their customary rights are not recognized in several countries").

protected areas. Paragraph 20 states that physical relocation should be avoided and is only an option in "exceptional circumstances, when it is not possible to avoid it…" In such exceptional circumstances, relocation may then only take place with indigenous peoples' broad community support subsequent to FPICon. If indigenous peoples do provide broad support, a resettlement plan, developed in accordance with OP 4.12 on Involuntary Resettlement, is required, which will be compatible with indigenous peoples' preferences and requires a land-based resettlement strategy.[60] A right of return once the reasons for resettlement have ceased should also be included in the plan.

While the potential of paragraph 20 to provide adequate protection for indigenous peoples' rights ultimately depends on what 'broad community support' means in practice, this paragraph is nonetheless a significant evolution in thinking within the Bank and especially when viewed in relation to the previous draft of OP 4.10 (dated 17 May 2004).[61] Not only have they ceased to use the term 'involuntary resettlement', this is the first time that the Bank has agreed that indigenous peoples have some degree of say about relocation and should broad support not exist that it will not fund the proposed project, at least the resettlement component (this could of course still be funded and take place outside of the Bank project itself and it remains to be seen how the Bank would address such a situation). On the other hand, 'feasible' probably still refers to economic feasibility as it will always be otherwise feasible to avoid relocation simply by not doing the project at all.

Paragraph 21 provides that involuntary restrictions on access to protected areas "should be avoided" except in exceptional circumstances where this is not feasible. Note that the term "involuntary" is employed as well as the absence of the term "broad community support" in relation to access restrictions, including potential restrictions to sacred areas. Where it is not feasible to avoid restrictions, the borrower prepares, with the FPICon of indigenous peoples, a process framework in accordance with OP 4.12.[62] This process framework is intended to result in the development of a management plan for a protected area and, according

---

[60] For requirements of a resettlement plan, see OP 4.12 on Involuntary Resettlement, December 2001 (revised April 2004), para. 6, available at http://wbln0018.worldbank.org/Institutional/Manuals/OpManual.nsf/0/ CA2D01A4D1BDF58085256B19008197F6?OpenDocument

[61] Supra note 15, para. 20 (providing that involuntary relocation may take place subsequent to "consultation" with indigenous peoples). See also, id. para. 9, which provides that:

> Bank experience has shown that resettlement of indigenous peoples with traditional land-based modes of production is particularly complex and may have significant adverse impacts on their identity and cultural survival. For this reason, the Bank satisfies itself that the borrower has explored all viable alternative project designs to avoid physical displacement of these groups. When it is not feasible to avoid such displacement, preference is given to land-based resettlement strategies for these groups (see para. 11) that are compatible with their cultural preferences and are prepared in consultation with them.

[62] OP 4.12, paragraph 7, provides that:

> 7. In projects involving involuntary restriction of access to legally designated parks and protected areas (see para. 3(b)), the nature of restrictions, as well as the type of measures necessary to mitigate adverse impacts, is determined with the participation of the displaced persons during the design and implementation of the project. In such cases, the borrower prepares a process framework acceptable to the Bank, describing the participatory process by which
> (a) specific components of the project will be prepared and implemented;
> (b) the criteria for eligibility of displaced persons will be determined;
> (c) measures to assist the displaced persons in their efforts to improve their livelihoods, or at least to restore them, in real terms, while maintaining the sustainability of the park or protected area, will be identified; and
> (d) potential conflicts involving displaced persons will be resolved.
>
> The process framework also includes a description of the arrangements for implementing and monitoring the process.

to paragraph 21, must "ensure that Indigenous Peoples participate in the design, implementation, monitoring and evaluation of the management plan, and share equitably in benefits…" Finally, the management plan "should give priority to collaborative arrangements" allowing indigenous peoples to continue to use resources in an "ecologically sustainable manner."

Paragraph 21 is troubling in a number of respects, most importantly because there has been a conscious choice to state that the envisaged restrictions will be "involuntary" and the failure to explicitly employ the term "broad community support". Also, the Bank is one of the implementing agencies for funds from the Global Environment Facility, and therefore plays a significant role in funding protected areas in all regions of the world. Some GEF projects have been heavily criticized by indigenous peoples for, sometimes, gross violations of their rights, including forced resettlement and unilateral expropriation of traditional lands and resources. Independent studies conducted by NGOs, academics and others confirm many of these allegations.[63]

Moreover, it appears that FPICon in paragraph 21 is only related to the development of a process framework rather than whether there are involuntary restrictions in the first place. It is however possible that the general requirements of FPICon and broad community support set forth in paragraphs 1, 6(c), 10 and 11 would apply to all projects and therefore that paragraph 21 only deals with involuntary restrictions subsequent to broad community support for the project in general. Nonetheless, it appears that the Bank has consciously created an exception to the broad community support requirement in this paragraph. It is also unclear whether protected areas would fall into either category (a) or (b) in paragraph 17 and therefore trigger the requirement that indigenous peoples' rights to lands, territories and resources be recognized and regularized prior to the establishment of protected areas.

If we apply the most negative interpretation of paragraph 21 it would appear to permit unilateral expropriation of indigenous peoples' lands, territories and resources in the name of nature conservation; non-consensual restrictions on access to protected areas including sacred areas located therein; and little more than participation in protected area management, which "should," rather than must, provide for continued use of resources. This paragraph, if this is the correct interpretation, also adds to the conclusion that OP 4.10 has not provided adequate protections for indigenous peoples' land and resource rights as the WBG committed to do in its response to the EIR.

The preceding 'worst case' interpretation is clearly contrary to indigenous peoples' rights in international law and contravenes the Convention on Biological Diversity. With regard to the former, the UN Human Rights Committee has emphasized that "securing continuation and sustainability of traditional forms of economy of indigenous minorities (hunting, fishing and gathering), and protection of sites of religious or cultural significance for such minorities …must be protected under article 27 [of the International Covenant on Civil and

---

[63] See, among others, T. Griffiths, *Indigenous Peoples and the Global Environment Facility (GEF). Indigenous Peoples' experiences of GEF-funded Biodiversity Conservation – A critical study*. Forest Peoples Programme, UK (January 2005), available at: http://www.forestpeoples.org/documents/ifi_igo/gef/gef_study_jan05_eng.pdf ; and K. Schmidt-Soltau, Conservation-related Resettlement in Central Africa: Environmental and Social Risks, Development and Change 34: 525-551 (2003).

4

Political Rights]."[64] Under the Convention on Biological Diversity,[65] legally binding Decision VII/28 on Protected Areas, adopted in 2004 by the 7th Conference of Parties, the Convention highest decision-making body, provides "that the establishment, management and monitoring of protected areas should take place with the full and effective participation of, and full respect for the rights of, indigenous and local communities consistent with national law and applicable international obligations."[66] This language clearly also requires full respect for indigenous peoples' rights in international human rights law ("applicable international obligations"). Additionally, pursuant to the Bank's Operational Policy 4.10 on Environmental Assessment, the Bank is enjoined from financing projects that contravene a borrower's obligations under international environmental law.[67] As of November 2004, the CBD has 182 parties, almost all of them members of the WBG, and is certainly part of the corpus of international environmental law.

B. Concluding remarks

While there are clear statements in OP 4.10 that the Bank will not process and finance projects unless indigenous peoples' communities have expressed their broad community support for a project in the initial stages of project processing – determined on the basis of, at a minimum, a social assessment and the outcome of a FPICon process – broad community support is not defined in any way; it is unclear whether or, if so when, it must be obtained in subsequent stages of the project or in relation to certain kinds of projects or project activities (i.e., involuntary restrictions to protected areas); it does not appear to be required at all in relation to the design of an IPP/IPPF; there is no mechanism for verification of and complaints about broad support; and, there are a number of problems related to the definitions of 'collective attachment' and 'forced severance' that may limit the applicability of the broad community support requirement. Additionally, the nature of and extent to which informed participation is required as part of FPICon, if at all, as distinct from mere consultation, is very unclear.

Although certain elements of the draft OP may be considered improvements over prior versions – the provision on physical relocation may fall into this category – the extent of some of these potential improvements, including that on relocation, ultimately turn on the definition of FPICon resulting in broad community support. Furthermore, the Bank's record of applying and adhering to its operational policies is poor and, assuming that an acceptable definition of FPICon resulting in broad community support is possible, its efficacy remains subject to implementation and enforcement mechanisms. That OP 4.10 does not contain prompt and simple mechanisms for indigenous peoples to challenge and complain about faulty or false assessments of broad community support nor require that such support and the conditions thereof be subject to written agreements between the borrower and affected indigenous peoples should be seen in this context. Without prompt and effective grievance, complaints and verification mechanisms, adherence to OP 4.10 is largely dependent on the good will of the borrower and the Bank.

---

[64] *Concluding observations of the Human Rights Committee: Australia. 28/07/2000. CCPR/CO/69/AUS. (Concluding Observations/Comments)*, at para. 8.

[65] Convention on Biological Diversity (June 5, 1992), *at* http://www.biodiv.org/doc/legal/cbd-en.pdf

[66] Decision VII/28 Protected Areas, at para. 22. In, *Decisions Adopted by the Conference of Parties to the Convention on Biological Diversity at its Seventh Meeting*. UNEP/BDP/COP/7/21, pps. 343-64.

[67] *See* OP 4.01 on Environmental Assessment and OP 4.36 on Forests.

III. The International Finance Corporation

The IFC is part of the private sector arm of the WBG and as such provides loans and other support to corporations and other private sector entities, including some of the world's wealthiest, rather than to governments. According to the IFC, its mission is "to promote sustainable private sector development in developing countries helping reduce poverty and improve peoples' [*sic*] lives. IFC believes that sound economic growth, grounded in sustainable private investment, is crucial to poverty reduction."[68] As the IFC often buys a stake in projects, it operates as both guarantor of environmental and social standards in projects and as an investor that stands to profit from the same projects.

The IFC has traditionally employed the safeguard policies used by the Bank, such as OD 4.20 on Indigenous Peoples. Citing the need to be more responsive to the needs of the private sector, particularly the differences in lending to the private as opposed to the public sector for which the safeguard policies were primarily designed, the IFC obtained Board approval to adopt a new set of safeguards in 2003. It subsequently proposed that the ten safeguard policies previously in use will be replaced by eight new 'performance standards' and an IFC Policy that will set out "IFC's roles and responsibilities in its investment operations, as well as the requirements that IFC's clients are expected to fulfil for IFC financing."[69] One of these performance standards addresses indigenous peoples.

The Performance Standards are complemented by the IFC's Policy on Social and Environment Sustainability, which sets forth the obligations of the IFC as distinct from requirements of clients contained in the Performance Standards, and by Guidance Notes, which contain non-binding principles of best practice that the client may or may not choose to follow. There is also a new IFC disclosure policy being developed that will define when and whether the IFC and client are required to disclose information to affected persons, communities or peoples, or to the general public. Given that policy requirements as well as best practice statements are spread over a number of documents and policies, the new IFC framework, at least as presently drafted, is confusing and it is sometimes difficult to ascertain with any specificity what is required in a given situation. Moreover, the IFC has allowed for a much higher degree of flexibility and discretion, both for itself and the client than is enjoyed under the existing policy framework without elaborating concomitant accountability measures. This raises serious questions about the degree to which IFC and clients can be held responsible for social and environmental problems caused by their activities.

The impact of the revision of the IFC's safeguard policies goes far beyond changes to the operating policies of the IFC itself. In the past three years more than 29 large commercial banks have agreed to follow a set of environmental and social standards known as the Equator Principles which are based on the IFC's safeguard policies.[70] These banks provided 80 percent (US$55.1 billion) of all private sector direct foreign investment financing around

---

[68] IFC Draft, at 2.

[69] *Id.*, at 1.

[70] *See The Equator Principles.* Available at: http://www.equator-principles.com

the world in 2003.[71] Further, national export credit agencies (ECAs) are increasingly relying on IFC safeguard standards. Both the Equator Banks and various ECAs will adopt the new IFC standards as their own once they come into force. As the IFC revises its own policies, it is in effect undertaking a global standard setting exercise affecting environmental and social issues in the vast majority of privately financed projects.

IFC-supported operations have greatly affected some indigenous peoples. The Chad-Cameroon oil pipeline project (also funded in part by the Bank), for instance, passes through indigenous lands in Cameroon and has resulted in uncompensated and non-consensual losses of lands and resources, exacerbated conflicts with non-indigenous neighbours, and has caused an overall deterioration in indigenous peoples' economic and social well-being. Protected areas established under the project to off-set biodiversity loss have also resulted in violations of indigenous peoples' rights. A number of IFC supported mining projects – the Glamis-operated mine in Guatemala and the Newmont-operated Yanacocha mine in Peru, for instance – have also engendered substantial opposition from affected indigenous peoples. Will the proposed new IFC performance standard on indigenous peoples provide effective safeguards and ensure that this will not occur in the future?

A. Performance Standard 7 on Indigenous Peoples

1. Objectives and application

4

As noted above the revised IFC safeguards include a performance standard on indigenous peoples ("PS7" or "the PS"). Other performance standards also affect indigenous peoples, for instance, PS5 on involuntary resettlement and PS8 on cultural resources. Similar to OP 4.10, the objectives of the PS7 are stated as: "to ensure that the development process fosters full respect for the dignity, human rights, aspirations, cultures and customary livelihoods of indigenous peoples;" to avoid or minimize risks to indigenous peoples occupying or using the affected area; to promote informed participation throughout the life of a project; to "foster good faith and meaningful engagement" with indigenous peoples when projects are to be located on traditional or customary lands; and to respect indigenous peoples' culture, knowledge and practices.[72] 'Engagement' is defined in PS1 as "disclosure of information, consultation, and informed participation, in a manner commensurate to the risks and impacts to the affected communities."

As with OP 4.10, PS7 does not employ a definition of the term 'indigenous peoples' as such observing that there is no accepted international definition. Instead it says that it will apply to indigenous peoples who are a "distinct social and cultural group" possessing the following characteristics in varying degrees

■ Self-identification as members of a distinct indigenous cultural group and recognition of this identity by others;

■ Collective attachment to geographically distinct habitats or ancestral territories in the project area and to the natural resources in these habitats and territories;

---

[71] *IFC Strategic Directions 2004*, International Finance Corporation: Washington D.C., 23 March 2004, 2. Available at: http://www.ifc.org/ifcext/about.nsf/AttachmentsByTitle/2004StrategicDirections/$FILE/2004StrategicDirectionsPaper.pdf

68   [72] IFC Draft, p. 25.

■ Customary cultural, economic, social, or political institutions that are separate from those of the dominant society or culture; and

■ An indigenous language, often different from the official language of the country or region.[73]

2. Impact assessment and related requirements

PS7 contains a number of requirements that the client must meet. Many of these requirements are related to and derived from the environmental and social impact assessment process required by and set forth in PS1. Therefore, PS7 should be read conjunctively with the requirements in PS1 and, the need for indigenous peoples' meaningful and informed participation in impact assessment processes is heightened. This is particularly the case because impact assessments undertaken without indigenous peoples' participation often mischaracterize, underestimate or omit impacts that should require attention under PS7 or other performance standards. It is unclear whether indigenous peoples' participation is required in impact assessment unless this requirement can be read into the following language in PS7, particularly the language "from as early as possible in the project planning…:"

> The client will establish an on-going relationship with the affected communities of Indigenous Peoples from as early as possible in the project planning through decommissioning of the project, through an on-going process to inform Indigenous Peoples of the risks and impacts that may be posed by the project, and to consult with and seek the informed participation of the Indigenous Peoples in decisions that affect them.

The non-binding Guidance Notes 14 and 20 to PS7 indicate that participation in impact assessment should be at least considered best practice, stating respectively that

> As part of the S&EA process, and as required by the Performance Standard, the client will engage with the affected communities of Indigenous Peoples within the project's area of influence through the process of information disclosure, consultation and informed participation. The general characteristics of engagement with affected communities are described in Performance Standard 1 and Guidance Note 1, and further described below as they apply to Indigenous Peoples in particular. Further guidance on engagement processes is provided in IFC's Good Practice Manual Doing Better Business through Effective Public Consultation and Disclosure.

> Clients should encourage participation of affected communities of Indigenous Peoples throughout the project in the process of project assessment and implementation. It is through an iterative process of listening to and incorporating concerns, sharing certain decisions, and adapting the project as necessary and feasible, that the project manages risks to the affected communities and improves its social performance. Engagement with the affected communities of Indigenous Peoples in important project decisions that may affect the interests of these communities should continue throughout the life of the project.

[73] Id., at 26.

Guidance Note 11 to PS7 also states that "Useful guidance on the conduct of cultural, environmental and social impact assessments can also be found in the Akwé: Kon Guidelines." The Akwé:Kon Guidelines provide detailed information on impact assessments related to projects affecting indigenous lands and territories and were developed with substantial input by indigenous peoples prior to their adoption by the Conference of Parties to the Convention on Biological Diversity in March 2004.[74] It would be better if the Akwé:Kon Guidelines were directly incorporated into PS7, or, at minimum, were recognized as best practice in the Guidance Notes.

3. Specific requirements

Specific requirements contained in PS7 include the following (the FPICon and broad community support requirements will be discussed in sub-section 4 below):

■ Client will identify indigenous peoples in the project's area of influence, as well as the nature and degree of the expected social, cultural (including cultural heritage), and environmental impacts on them and where possible avoid adverse impacts on indigenous peoples. Where avoidance is not possible, client will mitigate, minimize or compensate for adverse impacts.

This requirement should be viewed in light of the ambiguities surrounding indigenous peoples' right to informed participation in impact assessments in PS7. However, even with informed participation, the client's impact assessments need not respect and incorporate indigenous peoples' views and preferences, all that need occur is that these views are incorporated into the client's decision-making processes, which may reach conclusions contrary indigenous peoples' preferences. This conclusion is based on the IFC's own definition of 'informed participation' found is PS1, which states that "Informed participation involves organized and iterative consultation, leading to the client's incorporating into their decision-making process the views of the affected communities on matters that affect them directly, such as the design of mitigation measures, the sharing of development benefits and opportunities, and implementation issues."[75] This definition should be referenced wherever the term 'informed participation' is used on PS7 or elsewhere in the IFC framework (see, for instance, on Action Plans and development opportunities below).

The "project's area of influence" is defined in PS1 as:

(i) the primary project site(s) and related facilities that the client (including its contractors) develops or controls (e.g., power transmission corridors, pipelines, canals, tunnels, relocation and access roads, borrow and disposal areas, construction camps);

(ii) **associated facilities** that are not funded as part of the project (funding may be provided separately by the client or by third parties including the government), and whose viability and existence depends exclusively on the project and whose goods or services are essential for the successful operation of the project;

---

[74] *Akwe: Kon Guidelines for the Conduct of Cultural, Environmental and Social Impact Assessment Regarding Developments Proposed to Take Place on, or Which are Likely to Impact on, Sacred Sites and on Lands and Waters Traditionally Occupied or Used by Indigenous and Local Communities*, adopted by the 7th Conference of Parties to the Convention on Biological Diversity.

[75] IFC Draft, at 4

(iii) areas potentially impacted by **cumulative impacts** from further planned development of the project, any existing project or condition, and other developments that are realistically defined at the time the S&EA is undertaken; and

(iv) areas potentially affected by impacts from unplanned but predictable developments caused by the project that may occur later in time or at a different location. The area of influence does not include potential impacts that would occur without the project or independently of the project.[76]

■ Mitigation, minimization or compensation measures, among others, must be clearly set forth in an Action Plan (governed by PS1), which must be developed with indigenous peoples' informed participation, and in a time bound plan such as an Indigenous Peoples Development Plan (IPDP) or a community development plan with separate components for indigenous peoples if the projects affects a broader group of persons/communities;

The Action Plan is the primary instrument that governs the life of a project, whereas an IPDP most likely will be an elaboration of certain elements of an Action Plan as it relates to indigenous peoples. Certain elements of the Action Plan may also be included in the financing agreement, the primary legal agreement applicable to a project, between the IFC and a client. Failure to comply with those elements incorporated into the financing agreement may allow the IFC to suspend the project or require other remedial action for breach of contract. This however assumes that the IFC is willing to take such action and its willingness also should be viewed in light of the fact that IFC will most likely also be an investor in the project itself. Further, while the Action Plan must be developed with indigenous peoples' participation, no such requirement is stated for the IPDP, unless the IPDP is considered an integral part of the Action Plan and this is unclear in PS1 and PS7.

■ The client will establish an on-going relationship with the affected indigenous peoples from as early as possible in the project planning through decommissioning of the project, through an on-going, culturally appropriate process to inform indigenous peoples of risks and impacts that may be posed by the project, and to consult with and seek the informed participation of indigenous peoples in decisions that affect them. In particular, the process will:

   ■ Involve Indigenous Peoples' representative bodies (for example councils of elders or village councils, among others);

   ■ Be inclusive of both women and men and of various age groups in a culturally appropriate manner;

   ■ Provide for sufficient time for Indigenous Peoples' collective decision-making processes;

   ■ Facilitate the Indigenous Peoples' expression of their views, concerns, and proposals in the language of their choice; and

   ■ Ensure that the grievance mechanism or procedure established for the project, as described in Performance Standard 1, is culturally appropriate and accessible for Indigenous Peoples.

4

---

[76] *Id.* at 2.

4

The grievance mechanism referred to here is intended to act as a complaints mechanism and/or dispute resolution mechanism that will function at the project level. This most likely means that it will be an internal mechanism established and run by the client. It should not be viewed, however, as a substitute for recourse to national legal remedies, where these exist, or use of the IFC's complaints mechanism, know as the Compliance Advisor Ombudsman, should the complaint concern the failure of the IFC to comply with its responsibilities rather than the client specifically. The CAO performs largely the same function as the World Bank's Inspection Panel, receiving complaints about failures to adhere to safeguard policies.

- The client will provide development opportunities that are identified with the informed participation of the affected indigenous peoples. Such opportunities should be commensurate with the degree of project impacts, with the aim to improving their standard of living and livelihoods in a culturally appropriate manner, and to fostering the long-term sustainability of the natural resource on which they depend;

- If the project is to be located on traditional or customary lands under use, and adverse impacts can be expected on the customary livelihoods, and/or cultural, ceremonial or spiritual use that define the identity and community of the Indigenous Peoples, the client will respect their use by taking the following steps, in addition to the other requirements of this Performance Standard:

  - The client will document its efforts to avoid or at least minimize the size of land proposed for use by the project;

  - Indigenous peoples' land use will be documented by experts using appropriate methods in consultation with the affected communities of indigenous peoples;

  - The affected communities of indigenous peoples will be informed of their rights with respect to these lands under national law, including any national law recognizing any customary rights or use; and

  - The affected communities of indigenous peoples will be offered at least compensation and rights to due process available to those with full legal title to land in the case of commercial development of their land under national law, together with culturally appropriate development opportunities.

The first three of these points should all be part of an adequate environmental and social impact assessment and do not add much, if anything, to what a responsible company should be undertaking at present. Note also that, as with OP 4.10, PS7 focuses on only impacts to "customary livelihoods," rather than all livelihoods. As noted with respect to the OP, this formulation is discriminatory as non-indigenous persons' rights to their livelihoods are not limited only to those that are customary and many indigenous peoples' livelihoods today are at least in part something other than customary.

The last point potentially undervalues indigenous peoples' rights to and relationships with traditional lands, territories and resources, and undermines indigenous peoples' rights in international law. Indigenous peoples' rights to lands, territories and resources including attendant due process, cultural and other rights are not equivalent to the property rights of non-indigenous persons and are accorded higher degrees of protection under international law and some domestic legal regimes. One higher due process standard accorded to indigenous peoples' property rights under international law – at least in part because of the applicability of the right to self-determination – is the right to give or withhold FPIC, including in cases of compulsory acquisition or takings and proposed resettlement. This right does not apply to non-indigenous persons in international law. It is therefore not appropriate that indigenous property rights be treated in the same manner as non-indigenous property rights. Also, many companies will do only the minimum that is required to comply with external requirements resulting in indigenous peoples' being treated in same the manner as non-indigenous property holders. Finally, culturally appropriate development opportunities are required under other sections of PS7, therefore, the only requirement that this sections adds is one that undermines indigenous peoples' internationally guaranteed rights. The significance of this language further amplified in relation to PS5 and PS7 as they apply to economic displacement of indigenous peoples due to involuntary takings of lands for project purposes (see below).

■ "Care should be taken to ensure that any indigenous peoples' land claim is not prejudiced during these steps."

It is entirely unclear what the actual requirements are in relation to this statement and it is unclear how the term land claim may be understood and used in practice. In the first place, non-mandatory language 'should' is employed raising questions about whether the client is actually required to do anything pursuant to this section. Second, the term 'care' may imply a duty to exercise due diligence to verify if a 'land claim' exists (something that should be done as part of the impact assessment) or it may imply some other more or less onerous duty. With regard to ensuring that the client's actions will not prejudice the 'claim', the term 'prejudice' is highly contextual and open to various interpretations, many of which may not comport with indigenous peoples' views.

Use of the term 'claim' is also problematic in and of itself as indigenous peoples have rights in international law to own and control lands, territories and resources traditionally owned or otherwise occupied and used. States and corporations have, at a minimum, the obligation to respect those rights. Rights in this sense are not 'claims', but impose specific obligations of conduct and result applicable to others. Also, in principle any operation within indigenous peoples' traditional territories that takes place without their consent may be considered a violation of rights and this is certainly prejudicial to those rights or a 'claim' over the same lands. The next question, considering that indigenous peoples' rights are inherent, is whether a 'claim' must be cognizable under national law or even officially registered in order to be considered a 'claim' for the purposes of PS7?

The sentence in question refers only to avoiding prejudice "during these steps," meaning during the actions under the four bullet points in the preceding section. If prejudice were to occur in relation to informing indigenous peoples about rights under national law or in documenting land use, the client presumably will have acted dishonestly or incompetently. Point four is by itself prejudicial to indigenous peoples' rights and therefore it is difficult to see how the client could avoid additional prejudice. The only way to avoid prejudice under the first point, at least without FPIC by indigenous peoples, would be simply to avoid any use of or encroachment on indigenous lands, something that would preclude the further application of PS7 entirely. Finally, the Guidance Notes provide no help in clearing up any of these difficulties saying only that "Indigenous Peoples' claims to land or resources will be documented as part of the S&EA process."[77]

---

[77] *Id.* at 113, Guidance Note 24.

4

- The client will make every effort to avoid the relocation of Indigenous Peoples from their communally held traditional or customary lands under use. If relocation is unavoidable, the client will not proceed unless it enters into good faith negotiation with the affected indigenous peoples and documents their informed participation, consistent with PS7 and PS5 as it relates to physical displacement. The footnote associated with this section adds that "Where members of the affected communities of Indigenous Peoples individually hold legal title, or where the relevant national law recognizes customary rights for individuals, the requirements of Performance Standard 5 will apply, rather than the requirements under this heading." In other words, good faith negotiation and other requirements will not apply to indigenous persons holding individual rights.

The language pertaining to good faith negotiation as it relates to physical displacement/ relocation and cultural resources (see below), is discussed in the section on broad community support immediately following this section. Both the preceding section and PS5 cross reference each other and should be read conjunctively. PS 5 in particular states that when indigenous peoples are to be either physically or economically displaced, the requirements of PS7 must be followed as well as the requirements of PS5. In the case of physical relocation the above quoted language applies and should a negotiated settlement resulting in relocation be concluded, PS5 must then be reference for further requirements. In the case of economic displacement however there is no obligation for the client to reach a negotiated a settlement pursuant to either PS5 or PS7. As with OP 4.10, this may encompass involuntary restrictions on access to protected areas and takings of traditional indigenous lands, provided that physical displacement is not involved.

According to PS5, 'economic displacement' means the "loss of assets or access to assets that leads to loss of income sources or means of livelihood as a result of *project-related land acquisition*" (emphasis added). PS5 is clear that this may occur involuntarily including in the case of indigenous peoples. In defining its scope of application, PS5 specifies that it applies to land transactions that are for a private sector project acquired through expropriation or other "compulsory procedures" and; "for a private sector project acquired through negotiated settlements with property owners or those with legal rights to land, including customary or traditional rights recognized or recognizable under the laws of the country, who do not have the option to retain the land."

Consequently, under the proposed IFC standards it is permissible for a company, or the government on behalf of a company, to take indigenous peoples' traditional lands and territories, and as long as physical displacement is not involved to do no more than (as provided by PS7) seek their informed participation in decision making and offer compensation and rights to due process at least equal to that available to persons with full legal title to land. While PS7 does at least ensure that indigenous peoples will be treated as the equivalent of any title holder irrespective of whether they are recognized as such by national law – an improvement over the terms of PS5 apply to persons without formal legal title – non-consensual expropriation of indigenous peoples' lands and territories amounts to a gross violation of their internationally guaranteed rights.

- Where a project uses the cultural resources, knowledge, innovations, and/or practices of indigenous peoples for commercial purposes, the client will inform the Indigenous Peoples of (i) their rights under national law; (ii) the scope and nature of the proposed commercial development; and (iii) the potential consequences of such development.

Before proceeding with the commercial development, the client will enter into good faith negotiation with the affected indigenous people, document their informed participation, and provide for fair and equitable sharing of benefits of such knowledge, innovation, or practice, consistent with their customs and traditions.

4. FPICon and broad community support

While the FPICon and broad community support requirement is set out in various sections of OP 4.10, the requirement is not specifically stated at all in PS7. In order to understand how the principle operates in the IFC framework reference must be made to PS1 on impact assessment, the IFC Draft Procedure for Environmental and Social Review of Projects and the IFC Policy on Environmental and Social Sustainability, the latter two only applying to the IFC itself. These components of the policy framework are the only ones that explain and require FPICon and broad community support. As noted above, it is very likely that the Equator Banks and a number of ECAs will also adopt the IFC's new performance standards as their own operating policies. They will not however adopt the policies that only apply to the IFC. Therefore, the broad community support requirement – being absent from the performance standards – will not be included in policies adopted by the Equator Banks and ECAs, unless they choose to modify the IFC standards when they incorporate them into their own policies.

a. Defining FPICon and broad community support

According to PS1, "Broad community support is a collective expression by the affected communities, through individuals and/or their recognized representatives, in support of the project. There may be broad community support even if some individuals or groups object to the project."[78] The terms 'individuals' and 'groups' in the last sentence refer to persons or groups within a 'community' and therefore indicates that broad community support may be determined to exist despite the objections of small numbers of individuals or small groups within a 'community'. Two of the main questions raised by this definition are:

1) What is the 'community' for the purposes of broad community support – is it a village, the entire indigenous people(s) or some sub-entity, such as a clan, for instance – and will this account for indigenous peoples' customary laws which may assign rights in different circumstances to different entities: individuals, families, extended families, clans, villages, geographically defined sub-groups or the entire nation or people? In this context, also, are the 'recognized representatives' those recognized by indigenous peoples or by the state/national law?

2) If broad community support can exist over the objections of individuals or groups within the 'community', how much of the 'community' must be in support or opposed for broad community support to exist or not exist? What does this say about traditional consensus-based decision-making processes employed by indigenous peoples?

The IFC also provides a definition of FPICon, one that is substantially different from and less accommodating than that found in footnote 1 in OP 4.10. According to Guidance Note 45 to PS1, "Consultation should be 'free' (free of intimidation or coercion), 'prior' (timely

4

disclosure of information) and 'informed' (relevant, understandable and accessible information), and apply to the entire project process and not to the early stages of the project alone." This is no more than a description of the terms preceding the word 'consultation' and should be part of any consultation process at present.

b. Application of FPICon and broad community support

The major difference between the OP and IFC policy is that FPICon and broad community support is only required for **large** projects with **significant** adverse impacts under the IFC framework.[79] Under OP 4.10, FPICon and broad community support is required for **all** projects and at **each stage** of the project. This is a difference that is difficult to understand and justify, at least on the basis of any distinction between the nature of public and private sector projects. The only indication of the nature of a 'significant adverse impact' is found in the IFC's project categorization criteria, which indicate that such project impacts are "diverse, irreversible or unprecedented;" "may be partially mitigated or compensated, but cannot be completely avoided or fully mitigated;" and, "pose substantial risks to surrounding communities or environment."[80] Note also that if a project has such impacts but it is not further classified as a 'large' project, the FPICon and broad community support requirement is not applicable.

In addition to large projects with significant adverse impacts, PS7 most likely requires verified broad community support in relation to two other issues: relocation and the commercial use of cultural resources and traditional knowledge. This is not explicitly stated in PS7 although it is confirmed in the associated Guidance Notes and through personal communications with IFC staff. At least with regard to relocation, the Guidance Notes state that "IFC will evaluate the client's documentation of its engagement process to establish that broad community support for the relocation exists amongst affected communities."[81]

As stated in the preceding section, when relocation is unavoidable or where a project plans to commercially develop indigenous peoples' cultural resources or traditional knowledge, "the client will not proceed unless it enters into good faith negotiation with the affected indigenous peoples and documents their informed participation…" At least with regard to relocation, the logic employed by the IFC should be as follows: the client must negotiate the terms of relocation with affected indigenous peoples – should indigenous peoples agree, the next step will be for the client to develop a Resettlement Action Plan (as governed by PS1 and 5), which will be reviewed by IFC; however, if the negotiation between the client and indigenous peoples does not result in an agreement concerning resettlement, the IFC should acknowledge the failure to agree as evidence that broad community support does not exist and therefore decline to finance the project.

If the preceding is in fact what is required by PS7, it begs the question of why the IFC cannot clearly state this rather than only noting it in a non-mandatory Guidance Note. The language presently used in PS7 does not necessarily lead to the conclusion that broad community support or agreement subsequent to negotiation is required. It merely states that the client **will enter** into good faith negotiation without specifying any required result

---

[79] *Id.* at 3.

[80] *Id.* at 3 and Draft IFC Environmental and Social Review Procedures, at 4.2.2.

[81] *Id.* at 114, Guidance Note 28.

of the negotiation nor even that the negotiation has to have any result at all. As noted above, the requirement also only applies in cases of physical displacement but not to economic displacement. Moreover, the terms of a Resettlement Action Plan should be agreed to as part of the negotiations themselves not after the negotiations. This is the case because, assuming that the RAP does not simply codify the agreement reached in the negotiation, indigenous peoples' broad community support/agreement must be based on a full consideration of all relevant information, which includes the RAP.

While presumably negotiation must be with recognized representatives of the affected indigenous people(s), employing a negotiation process rather than an explicitly community-based decision-making process – such as FPIC or perhaps even broad community support – fails to acknowledge substantial inequalities in bargaining power among the parties and the heightened possibilities for manipulation of the process. To address the last point, at a minimum, PS7 could specify and require that any negotiated settlement be ratified by the affected community/people as an integral part of the negotiation process and that it be independently verified to further guard against coercion or manipulation. Presumably indigenous peoples may insist on this in discussions with the client, but the client is not required to agree with this, and may be reluctant to do so particularly if manipulation of the process or coercion is involved.

Finally, given that the IFC sometimes invests in projects that have commenced a number of years prior to its involvement, it is possible that project could involve relocation prior to IFC investment. The Guidance Notes acknowledge this situation and provide that:

> In cases where the host government has made the decision to relocate Indigenous Peoples, consultation with relevant government officials would be important to understand the rationale for such relocation, and whether a good faith negotiation based on informed participation of the Indigenous Peoples has been implemented regarding the aspects of the project and the relocation affecting communities of Indigenous Peoples, prior to the decision to finance the project.[82]

It is unclear what the result of such a retroactive analysis would be and this paragraph fails to state what action the client or the IFC should take if it is determined that good faith negotiation did not take place. Without a clear statement on this issue, it may create an incentive for governments and companies to forcibly relocate indigenous peoples prior to seeking support from the IFC (the same could also be the case in relation to the Bank under OP 4.10). Given that this language is found in the Guidance Notes, it appears that it is the client, at its discretion, rather than the IFC that should review the manner in which relocation took place. However, it is also possible that this is something the IFC, again at its discretion, should do as the Guidance Note says that this should be done "prior to the decision to finance the project," which is the role of the IFC rather than the client.

c. Verification of broad community support

The OP and IFC policy frameworks are similar in that both require that the Bank and IFC respectively verify that broad community support exists as a precondition to financing the project. The IFC, for instance, states that:

IFC will review the client's documentation of the engagement process, and in addition, through its own investigation, assure itself that the client's community engagement is one that involves free, prior and informed consultation and enables the informed participation of the affected communities, leading to broad community support for the project within the affected communities, before presenting the project for approval by IFC's Board of Directors.[83]

The IFC's Draft Environmental and Social Review Procedures, which contain the procedures IFC staff are required to follow when processing projects, provides very little information on how the IFC will conduct its "own investigation" to assure itself that broad community support exists. It simply states that IFC's Environment and Social Department will "Support the [Transaction Leader*] in determining, in the case of large projects with significant adverse impacts, whether the project has Broad Community Support."[84] For both the IFC and the Bank, no independent verification is required nor is any specific written confirmation or refutation by indigenous peoples required to demonstrate that broad community support exists or does not exist. Moreover, both the Bank and IFC will rely primarily, at least initially, on documentation produced by the borrowing government and the client, or consultants hired by the government and client, to determine if broad community support exists.

B. Concluding Remarks

The proposed IFC policy framework and PS7 in particular are fraught with problems, loopholes and ambiguities that render their effectiveness as meaningful safeguards for indigenous peoples questionable at best. In many cases, the framework seems to be based on the implicit proposition that indigenous peoples should trust the IFC (and in some cases the client) to ensure that rights and interests are protected. In other cases, it is clear that PS7 does not provide an effective guarantee at all for rights and interests as the text permits activities that are in direct contravention of those rights and interests.

The same problems (and more) as those identified in OP 4.10 exist with regard to FPICon and broad community support and the provisions pertaining to lands, relocation and procedural issues are weak, vague and flawed. In some cases, PS7 is weaker than the standards set forth in OP 4.10. With regard to the last point, a Bank memorandum to the IFC concerning the draft IFC safeguards also notes that PS7 is inconsistent with and weaker that OP 4.10.[85] The forgoing should be viewed in the context of an increasing focus on the private sector as development actors and the well documented problems faced by indigenous peoples with many private sector projects. While the IFC may argue that its involvement should decrease these problems, the evidence suggests that this has not necessarily been the case in the past, nor, based on a review of the proposed standards, will it be in the future.

---

* The Transaction Leader is the member of IFC's Investment Department with overall responsibility for developing a particular project with a client. It corresponds to a Task Manager at the Bank.

[83] *Id.* at 4.

[84] *Draft IFC Environmental and Social Review Procedures*, Working Draft, Version 0.1, 22 September 2005, at 3.2.9. Available at: www.ifc.org/policyreview

[85] See, *Memorandum of Ian Johnson, EESD World Bank, to Asaad Jabre, IFC*, 5 August 2005, available at: http://www.ifc.org/ifcext/policyreview.nsf/AttachmentsByTitle/IFC+Response+and+ESSD+letter/$FILE/IFC+Cover+Note+_ESSD+Memo_.pdf

Finally, it must be considered that IFC has to date only held one formal meeting (in May 2005) with indigenous peoples to discuss its proposed new safeguard standards and that this meeting only focused on a draft that was said not to reflect the full views of IFC management and was received by the participants a few hours before the meeting. Moreover, the IFC only considered directly consulting with indigenous peoples when indigenous peoples themselves and a few NGOs complained about their exclusion from the revision process. This should be contrasted with the consultation process employed in relation to OP 4.10, which, although far from adequate and acceptable, involved numerous meetings with indigenous peoples, at the regional as well as the global levels. These consultations took place over more than nine years. The IFC should be held to account for this substantial failure to adhere to what has become an accepted practice of direct consultations with freely chosen indigenous representatives when policies are being revised or changed. These issues are discussed in greater detail in the next section.

IV. Indigenous peoples' engagement with the WBG

While indigenous peoples' have been affected by the activities of the WBG from the earliest days of its operations, other than in relation to a few localized projects, sustained engagement is relatively recent, dating initially from the late 1980s to the early 1990s. Around this time, indigenous peoples highlighted the need for major reforms within the WBG to ensure compliance with safeguard policies and demanded direct participation in the drafting of OD 4.20. They also proposed that WBG projects be subject to tripartite agreements between the WBG, the borrower or client, and indigenous peoples where these projects would affect traditional territories. In 1990, indigenous peoples from the Amazon demanded not only direct participation in drafting of the OD but also, among others, that it be consistent with indigenous rights in international law, that no projects be financed without prior consent and the prioritization of indigenous peoples' own development initiatives.[86] These same demands were reiterated by the International Alliance of Indigenous and Tribal Peoples of the Tropical Forests in 1992.[87]

Despite these demands, OD 4.20 was drafted internally by the Bank without any participation by or consultation with indigenous peoples. The same was also the case for OMS 2.34 adopted in 1982. As noted above, the process leading to the adoption of OP 4.10 was quite different and involved numerous meetings with indigenous peoples, both locally and globally. Nonetheless, this process was far from adequate and was severely criticized by indigenous peoples.[88] For instance, it was only after the revision process had been underway for four years that the first set of consultation meetings were held with indigenous peoples in 1998. These meetings focused on an 'approach paper' developed internally by Bank staff and were held in Brazil, Costa Rica, Ecuador, Viet Nam, Philippines, India and Russia.

---

[86] *IWGIA Yearbook 1990*, IWGIA: Copenhagen, 71.

[87] *Charter of the Indigenous-Tribal Peoples of the Tropical Forests 1992*, article 25.

[88] The revision process pertaining to OP 4.10 as well as other WBG processes affecting indigenous peoples are discussed in detail in, T. Griffiths, *Indigenous peoples and the World Bank: experiences with participation*, Forest Peoples Programme, UK (July 2005), available at: http://www.forestpeoples.org/documents/ifi_igo/wb_ips_and_particip_jul05_eng.pdf

4

A first draft of OP 4.10 was released for comment in 2001 and was followed by 25 meetings in 14 countries. While the Bank expressed considerable pride at its consultation efforts, indigenous peoples who participated reported numerous negative experiences and complained that the process was seriously flawed. For instance, 11 of the 25 meetings lasted less than one day and were reportedly mostly taken up by presentations by Bank staff leaving little time for discussion; some participants were not given the required documents until a few hours before the meeting; and, some meetings lacked adequate translation services.

In relation to the consultation process in general, indigenous peoples were also told by the Bank that their key demands expressed during the discussion of the approach paper could not be incorporated into the revised policy and few changes would be made to the text of the draft OP. While subsequent statements by the Bank back-tracked somewhat on this position, this view seems to be a common feature of consultations: indigenous peoples expect that issues and concerns raised will be reflected in ongoing revisions of text or project design, whereas the WBG is of the view that consultation does not require incorporation of indigenous peoples' views. However, this is not restricted only to processes involving indigenous peoples as the WBG similarly rejected recommendations, including those pertaining to indigenous peoples, such as respect for FPIC, made by the World Commission on Dams and the Extractive Industry Reviews, both of which were processes either initially commissioned by the WBG itself or in which it played a major role.

Additional meetings were held with Bank staff prior to the adoption of the OP in May 2005, including a legal roundtable with Bank lawyers and high ranking officials in 2002, and a meeting during the 2004 session of the Permanent Forum on Indigenous Issues session.[89] A statement issued by indigenous peoples in relation to the legal roundtable stated, among others, that "indigenous peoples do not accept the World Bank's March 2001 revised Draft Indigenous Peoples Policy (OP/BP4.10) as an effective instrument for safeguarding the rights and interests of indigenous peoples affected by its development projects and programmes;" and, "that we as indigenous peoples consider that we have so far been denied the opportunity to significantly shape the outcome of the policy revision and that the Bank has not addressed our principal concerns and our proposals on how to improve the existing policy."[90]

Serious concerns have also been raised in relation to OP 4.10 subsequent to its adoption. For instance, a statement endorsed by 25 indigenous organizations and presented to the UN Permanent Forum on Indigenous Issues in May 2005 states that:

---

[89] The discussions held at the legal roundtable are summarized in, M. Castello, *World Bank Round Table Discussion of Indigenous Representatives and the World Bank on the Revision of the World Bank's Indigenous Peoples Policy. Summary Report.* Forest Peoples Programme, UK (2003), available at http://www.forestpeoples.org/documents/ifi_igo/ wb_ip_round_table_summary_oct_02_eng.pdf

[90] *Indigenous Peoples' Statement to a Round Table Discussion on the Revision of the World Bank Policy on Indigenous Peoples,* 18 October 2002, available at: http://www.forestpeoples.org/documents/ifi_igo/ wb_ip_round_table_ip_statement_oct02_eng.shtml

The World Bank recently approved its Operational Policy on indigenous peoples (OP/BP 4.10) after seven years of consultations and revisions. ...

The newly revised policy has made important improvements in several areas, such as requiring that the commercial development of affected indigenous peoples' cultural resources and knowledge be conditioned upon their prior agreement to such development. Nevertheless, we continue to be extremely concerned about these Multilateral Development Banks lack of recognition of indigenous peoples' customary rights to their lands territories and natural resources and to their related right of free prior informed consent, and their derogation of international standards to national law. ...

Of specific concern is the World Bank's recent decision to require a process of free prior and informed consultation with affected indigenous peoples' communities to ascertain their broad community support for a project, rather than requiring the free prior and informed consent of the affected indigenous people. By merely requiring the World Bank to verify that the borrower has gained the "broad support from representatives of major sections of the community"– with no guarantees as to what information will be disclosed and when, how such verification will be conducted and by who, and how the collective decision-making processes and structures of the affected indigenous people will be recognized and respected – the free prior and informed consultation process stands to reduce indigenous peoples rights to a mere technical procedure. The weakening of free prior and informed consent as an international standard for indigenous peoples stands to severely threaten the lands, territories, and natural resources of indigenous peoples and to undermine their internationally recognized human rights.[91]

This same statement also called on the Bank "to create a mechanism which will guarantee the full and effective participation of indigenous peoples in discussing and defining the meaning and application of conducting free prior and informed consultation and ascertaining broad community support with the Bank's management, legal counsel, and task teams (TT). Indigenous peoples' suggestions and comments should be reflected in the forthcoming Indigenous Peoples Guidebook and in any revisions made to BP 4.10."[92]

While the process leading to the adoption of OP 4.10 was far from adequate, it certainly was an improvement in relation to the adoption of OMS 2.34 and OD 4.20. It should also be contrasted with the process employed by the IFC as it revises its safeguard framework. As noted above, in the almost three years since the process began, the IFC has held only one formal meeting, in May 2005, with indigenous peoples to discuss its policy. This meeting was largely off-the-record; hastily organized with participants not receiving the documents until a few hours before the meeting; and did not deal with text that had been endorsed by IFC management with the result that many questions were simply deferred and unanswered. The May 2005 statement to the Permanent Forum quoted above, therefore:

---

[91] *Multilateral Development Banks (MDBs) and Indigenous Peoples' Rights, including Free, Prior Informed Consent*, Statement to the Fourth Session of the UN Permanent Forum on Indigenous Issues (May 2005), available at: http://www.forestpeoples.org/documents/ifi_igo/wb_4_10_ip_statemnt_may05_eng.shtml

[92] *Id.*

Encourages the International Finance Corporation to conduct further consultations with indigenous peoples regarding the revision of its Performance Standards to ensure that indigenous peoples are able to provide recommendations as to how free prior and informed consent must be ascertained, and under which conditions, so as to ensure that indigenous peoples' customary land and natural resource rights are not undermined by the IFC and its private sector clients.[93]

Despite this call and despite the fact that a revised draft was released in September 2005 and is scheduled for final adoption in January 2006, the IFC has yet to initiate any formal consultation process with indigenous peoples' representatives to discuss PS7 and other components of the draft policy framework. Additionally, as discussed in section III above, the application of PS5 and PS7 will result in indigenous peoples' customary lands and natural resource rights being undermined and violated.

Indigenous peoples' experiences at the project level have not been much better than they have with policy processes, although there is some amount of variation depending on the nature of the project, the government involved and the degree to which indigenous peoples are organized in relation to the project. These projects have sometimes engendered substantial opposition by indigenous peoples and violent suppression of this opposition by some governments. Problems can and have occurred at all stages of projects: preparation, implementation, monitoring and closure, for example. Project preparation and design control the remainder of the project and, therefore, are the stages where indigenous peoples' input is most critical. According to Griffiths, however, it "is not uncommon for indigenous communities to only learn of a project once it has already started after key assumptions [have been] made and decisions taken by outsiders."[94] Put another way, many projects may be and are viewed as top-down, external interventions that are imposed on indigenous peoples, do not take into account their rights, priorities and preferences, and more often than not place the majority of costs on indigenous peoples while the vast majority of benefits are enjoyed by others.

The preceding views are largely confirmed by internal WBG studies. A 2003 review of the implementation of OD 4.20, for instance, observed that the participation of indigenous peoples in decision-making in WBG projects affecting them was "low" and that just 20 percent of projects had included clear benchmarks to measure impacts on indigenous communities.[95] The same report also found that sustainability of results for indigenous peoples in all project types was also generally much lower than overall project sustainability indicators.[96] Another internal report reviewing OD 4.20 in relation to 87 projects approved after 2001 found that around 20 percent had little or no provision for enabling indigenous peoples' participation.[97] Of those that did have participation measures, the report concluded that these were normally confined to basic consultation meetings rather than meaningful participation.[98]

---

[93] *Id.*

[94] Griffiths, *supra* note 88, at 13.

[95] OED Report No. 25332, *supra* note 18, at 20.

[96] *Id.* at 36.

[97] OED Report No. 25754, *supra* note 18, at 11.

[98] *Id.* at 20.

Finally, internal and external reviews have found that the entire safeguard system suffers from serious problems, both with regard to the substance of the policies as well as the institutional structures concerned with implementation and compliance. The Extractive Industries Review, for instance, concluded that "The reality in the field suggests that the current Safeguard Policies have been unable to ensure that 'no harm is done' and that this is due to both poor implementation rates and deficiencies in the policies themselves."[99] In reaching this conclusion the EIR in part relied on a 2002 general WBG evaluation of safeguard policies, which revealed that "performance in the area of safeguards has been only partially satisfactory. Fundamental reform of implementation and accountability processes is crucial. ...The current system does not provide the appropriate accountability structure to meet the WBG's commitments to incorporate environmental sustainability into its core objectives and to mainstream the environment into its operations."[100]

With regard to the then-draft OP 4.10, the EIR also concluded that "To be legitimate and effective, a Safeguard Policy must be seen by the intended beneficiaries to provide adequate safeguards and must be consistent with their internationally guaranteed rights. This is presently not the case [with draft OP 4.10]."[101] Highlighting the importance of attention to indigenous peoples' rights in relation to OP 4.10, the EIR's Eminent Person's, Dr. Emil Salim, stated that "the revision of the safeguard policy on indigenous peoples is a fundamental test of the World Bank's commitment to poverty alleviation through sustainable development."[102]

In a few projects, designated as ethno-development or 'do good projects' by the Bank and which targeted indigenous peoples in Latin America, indigenous peoples have acknowledged a higher degree of participation in and satisfaction with project design and results. According to Griffiths, improved performance in these projects was related to "long project preparation times, intensive staff inputs, willingness to pay unusually high transaction costs, strong borrower commitments to reform and genuinely participatory decision-making both in project preparation and implementation."[103] This could lead to the conclusion that these elements should all be part of any project affecting indigenous peoples. Nevertheless, even these projects have their critics, who argue that the projects have caused divisions in indigenous organizations and communities, failed to address underlying causes of poverty and have not effectively carried out the legal and policy reforms required to secure and protect indigenous peoples' land and resource rights.[104]

In order to comply with WBG safeguard policies, projects normally must have built-in participation mechanisms. Under OP 4.10 and to a lesser extent the IFC's draft policy framework, indigenous peoples' broad community support will now also be required in relation to projects. How this will work in practice and whether it will improve indigenous peoples' participation in, acceptance of and benefits derived from WBG projects remains

---

[99] EIR Report, *supra* note 3, at 37.

[100] A. Liebenthal, *Promoting Environmental Sustainability in Development: An Evaluation of World Bank Performance.* Washington DC: World Bank 2002, at 21, 24.

[101] EIR Report, at 41.

[102] Letter of Dr. Emil Salim to J. Wolfensohn, President of the World Bank, 12 January 2004. Available at: http://www.eireview.org/doc/Letter%20to%20Wolfensohn%2012%20Jan%202004-final.doc

[103] *Supra* note 88, at 16.

[104] *Id.* at 15-16.

to be seen. However, somewhere around 50 percent of World Bank operations is programmatic lending such as structural adjustment and technical assistance loans, which are not subject to the normal array of safeguard policies applying to projects, including those pertaining to indigenous peoples. Programmatic lending therefore also is not subject to any requirements concerning participation by indigenous peoples. These loans, which often have significant and long-lived negative impacts, are routinely designed and implemented behind closed doors and without any involvement of indigenous peoples or others.

In recent years, the Bank has begun to work through Poverty Reduction Strategy Papers with the goal of creating an alternative to traditional adjustment loans. While PRSP formulation processes do often require indigenous participation, indigenous peoples still complain that these processes disregard their concerns and still focus on conventional adjustment measures such as liberalization, increasing foreign investment and privatization. In some countries, indigenous peoples are not formally included in the process and are instead categorized simply as 'poor people' and lumped in with civil society in general. In others, indigenous peoples have managed to insert provisions in the PRSP, yet nonetheless maintain that these provisions are not implemented while the conventional adjustment-related provisions are prioritized.

The preceding indicates that there are major challenges to be faced when considering the nature and extent of future engagement with the WBG, be it at a policy, project or programme level. While some gains have been made in the past, these gains are tenuous, some exist mostly on paper, and others have yet to be tested in the real world, in particular in projects where governments are not committed to indigenous participation and rights. Additionally, some of what may be considered to be gains – the inclusion of broad community support, for instance – may actually represent serious set backs for indigenous peoples' rights in the long term. This will be especially the case if donor agencies, the private sector and other multilateral agencies, for example, adopt FPICon leading to broad community support in place of FPIC, the latter being employed by human rights bodies and some multi- and bilateral donors and private sector bodies. This is not far fetched as it is highly probable that the Equator Banks and a number of ECAs will adopt this terminology as part of incorporating IFC standards.

V. Conclusions and strategic issues

When thinking about how to deal with the institutions that comprise the WBG, the fact that they are owned and controlled by states should always be borne in mind. While consensus decision-making at the board level of the institutions often has the effect of softening extreme positions put forth by certain states, many of the states bring the same issues, concerns and prejudices about indigenous peoples to WBG decisions that they hold in domestic affairs. In some cases, policies expressed at the WBG may be less favourable to indigenous peoples than domestic policies because it is finance ministries or their equivalents that are the primary domestic focal points in relation to the WBG. These ministries sometimes adopt positions that are at odds with the positions and policies of ministries or agencies that address indigenous issues and the latter are normally not involved in formulating positions expressed at the WBG.

The dynamics of decision-making at the WBG are further complicated by the fact that all but five of the Executive Directors represent groups of states on the board and must achieve consensus among these groups prior to expressing a position at board meetings. This can also lead to the adoption of positions that contradict national policies and even national laws being expressed on behalf of certain countries. The Philippines, for instance, is represented at present by a Brazilian Executive Director. During the debate about FPIC at the WBG board meeting held in August/September 2004, this Executive Director was one of the most vigorous opponents of FPIC despite recognition of the right in the domestic law of the Philippines. Moreover, if it were so inclined, Philippines would be unable to dissociate itself from such a view at the level of the board or to express a contrary view on its own.

While the board is the ultimate authority in the WBG, the role of WBG staff and especially management should not be minimized. Projects and policies are in the first place designed by staff and endorsed by management. WBG staff thus has a substantial role in shaping what is eventually submitted to the board and the board, normally after substantial informal and formal interaction with staff and sometimes even negotiation with management, often makes few significant changes to what has been developed and forwarded by staff. In this respect, it is also important to bear in mind that WBG staff overall remains heavily dominated by economists, who often have little understanding of social and environmental issues. Understanding of human rights issues and the role of human rights in development is also minimal.

Moving from WBG policy issues to actual projects the situation can be equally complicated because projects are basically government or corporate initiatives that receive funding from the WBG. In the process of developing projects, the practice within the WBG, although much more so in the case of the Bank, seems to be to negotiate project development and conditions with the government and client with varying degrees of attention to safeguard policy issues. This sometimes leads to safeguards being applied (or not applied) in very different ways in different countries, something that will become even more complex if the Bank begins to systematically employ the use of country systems (meaning national laws) in place of safeguard policies.

The issue of the application of safeguards is further confused by the practice of the Bank and sometimes the IFC not to fund more than one-third of the total project costs. This often requires that additional donors be brought in as co-financers. These additional donors may be other development banks, UN agencies, bilateral donors, ECA's or the private sector, some or all of whom may have their own safeguard standards. This may then require a working knowledge or two, three or more sets of (potentially contradictory) policy standards that apply to one project as well as any complaints or grievance mechanisms that may be associated with the various policies. This problem is sometimes avoided by all donors agreeing to apply one donors safeguard standards, but this is not always the case. With regard to IFC projects it is also important to ascertain if the company in question employs specific internal policies and how these may relate to indigenous peoples.

With the preceding in mind, this final section provides thoughts and suggestions concerning future strategic engagement with the WBG, both at the policy and project levels, as well as engagement with other institutions and fora that may enhance the efficacy of future engagement with the WBG. In formulating these suggestions, I have tried to

4

ensure that they are general enough for adaptation to a variety of local situations and to thinking about a regional approach to these important issues. At the same time, given that there will be discussion of these issues in workshops and further elaboration of ideas and strategies, I have also tried to include mostly basic rather than detailed suggestions.

A. Policy level

OP 4.10 was adopted a mere six months ago and only applies to projects that entered the funding pipeline after August 2005. It therefore does not apply to the majority of Bank projects being developed and implemented. However, all projects that meet this time line need to be identified and carefully reviewed against the new standards contained in OP 4.10. One of the most important is clearly FPICon resulting in broad community support, particularly given the ambiguities surrounding this concept and the fact that its interpretation and utility may be strengthened and enhanced through practice in implementation or the opposite may be the case. The board of the Bank also committed to conducting a review of the first three years of implementation of OP 4.10, which will be carried out sometime in mid- to late-2008.

Bearing in mind that some indigenous peoples are opposed to and reject any engagement with the WBG, suggestions relating to OP 4.10 include:

- Ensuring that indigenous organizations, peoples and communities that are concerned with or may be affected by Bank projects are well informed about the requirements of OP 4.10 (and inter-connected OPs such as OP 4.01 on environmental assessment) and are able to insist that projects are at least consistent therewith. This is best done through direct training and the development of simple explanations of or guides to the Bank and its OPs with a special emphasis on OP 4.10. This training process should not treat Bank policy and projects in isolation from international human rights standards applicable to indigenous peoples;

- Establishing national and regional 'working groups' or the like to systematically identify and track Bank projects applying OP 4.10 with the aim of providing well documented inputs to the three year review of the OP agreed to by the board. In the same vein, these groups could advocate, together with indigenous peoples from other regions, for full indigenous participation in the three year review;

- Consistent with statements made to the UN Permanent Forum, advocating that the Bank establish or cooperate with mechanisms "which will guarantee the full and effective participation of indigenous peoples in discussing and defining the meaning and application of conducting free prior and informed consultation and ascertaining broad community support with the Bank's management, legal counsel, and task teams." One mechanism that the Bank could cooperate with in this respect is the UN Permanent Forum itself, which has begun work on FPIC methodology and mainstreaming FPIC in UN system activities pertaining to indigenous peoples;

- Irrespective of whether the Bank agrees to the preceding point, it is important for indigenous peoples, nationally, regionally and globally to proactively seek to define FPICon and broad community support in ways that are consistent with indigenous peoples' traditional (or otherwise prevailing and accepted) methods of collective

4

decision making and use these 'definitions' both as a means of working with affected communities/peoples and as a way of influencing government and Bank understanding and implementation of the concept in Bank-financed projects;

- With regard to the last point above and in general, it is important to identify those in government with primary responsibility for Bank projects and policy issues and attempt to influence their thinking. In some cases, this may be helped by involving national agencies and bodies responsible for indigenous issues or even legislative committees or other bodies in any dialogue. The wisdom of such an approach is very much dependent however on local political and other realities;

- In principle, Bank-funded project have to respect national laws. In some countries, national laws contain higher levels of protection for indigenous peoples' rights than OP 4.10. The Philippines' Indigenous Peoples' Rights Act is one such law, requiring FPIC and having, at least on paper, much higher protections for land and resource rights as the trigger for FPIC. In such countries, particular attention is required to assessing projects in relation to higher national legal standards in addition to OP 4.10 and in this sense it may be important to develop tailored training materials that focus on this aspect of Bank projects;

- A working relationship with the Indigenous Peoples' Unit at the Bank could also be useful in relation to all of the above as well as in general;

- Where a Bank project fails to adhere to the broad community support requirement or fails to apply the concept in an adequate manner, consideration could be given, where applicable, to filing a formal complaint with the Inspection Panel to seek a formal ruling on the nature and content of the concept (the risk would be that the Inspection Panel interprets the concept restrictively);

- Continue to provide input to and seek recommendations from the UN Permanent Forum with regard to the activities of Bank and interpretation and implementation of OP 4.10. Regional caucuses are the norm at the Permanent Forum and therefore, consideration can be given to formulating a regional position on OP 4.10 for discussion in the Asian caucus.

The IFC policy framework is still in draft form and although it is expected to be approved in January 2006, approval may take much longer. This makes it difficult to state concrete suggestions other than ones that pertain to the process of further elaborating the draft text and eventually its approval, or ones that apply to issues that almost certainly will appear in the final policy. Some of these are similar to those discussed above in relation to OP 4.10. I will begin with process issues:

- While there is not much time to do so, it is still important to submit national and regional statements expressing indigenous peoples' views on the IFC policy framework. At this time, this is best done by directing comments to Executive Directors rather than IFC staff, although until 25 November 2005, it is still possible to submit written comments electronically to the IFC. Comments to Executive Directors should be submitted not only to Asian Executive Directors but to all the Executive Directors, and could focus on the lack of meaningful consultations with indigenous peoples as well as flaws with the substance. It is also important to raise these issues with Permanent Forum members and ask that they reiterate concerns to the IFC and others;

■ The Equator Banks have a working group on the IFC policy revision process that provides input to the process as well as assesses implications for the Banks themselves. It is important to consider direct engagement with this group in order to seek strengthening of policy standards when these are incorporated into the common standards employed by the banks. This can be done using largely the same analysis as that employed for the IFC policy and in cooperation with sympathetic organizations monitoring the Equator Banks, such as the Bank Track Network. It is important to recall that these banks provide substantially more private sector financing than the IFC does and have expressed a willingness to address gaps in the IFC policy when they formulate or finalize their own standards;

■ The points proposed in the section on OP 4.10 could all also apply to the IFC policy once adopted.

B. Project level

Projects present some of the same issues that were raised above in relation to policies – after all the policies apply primarily to projects – as well as some different issues. Interpretation and application of broad community support is one very important issue in relation to projects and policies, for instance. There will also be differences in the way an IFC project may be approached compared to a Bank project given that the former invariably involves private sector actors. Key suggestions include:

■ Providing support to national and regional organizations to develop staff capacity to identify, advise affected communities on and monitor WBG-financed projects from as early in the project cycle as possible. Identifying projects early in the cycle is critical to success in influencing project design and subsequent implementation. A good understanding of the internal project processing cycle within the Bank is very important in this respect. As the project is designed through interactions between the government and the Bank, interventions should be addressed to both the Bank and government, although it may be strategic or, in some cases, the only option to focus more on the Bank and its compliance with safeguard policies – the only real means of holding the WBG accountable – if the government is inaccessible or unreceptive;

■ Consultants are usually employed in the design of projects and it is also therefore important to try to identify and communicate with consultants, particularly those specifically addressing indigenous peoples' issues and legal issues;

■ It is also important to identify the full range of financers in WBG-funded projects, whether they have policies of their own and to what extent these apply to the project in question. It is also important to communicate concerns to all of the donors involved as one may raise issues with the Bank or the government and can assist in influencing the project in this way. It is not uncommon for certain donors to take and act on more supportive positions in relation to indigenous peoples' rights than the WBG and the government or client and this possibility should not be ignored;

- In IFC projects, it is important to identify company policies that may apply to indigenous peoples and also compare these to project criteria and performance. The company may also be a member of an industry group that has policies that can be raised, for instance, the International Business Leaders Forum or the International Council on Metals and Mining. These policies, with the exception of company policies, are almost always voluntary and therefore of limited utility. Pressure can also be brought to bear on companies through shareholder meetings and through investor groupings with an interest in the company;

- Finally, where national legal systems provide adequate remedies, strategic litigation against WBG projects could form part of an overall strategy for addressing deficits in rights protection. While domestic remedies may not always be sufficient to achieve adequate rights protection, litigation may nonetheless be useful as a means of exhausting local remedies for the purposes of having the case reviewed by an international human rights body. This option, however, is only available to indigenous peoples in those countries that have ratified the relevant human rights instruments and/or accepted the jurisdiction of human rights bodies to receive complaints.

This is an important strategic option over and above addressing specific cases because building a body of jurisprudence demonstrating that rights violations occur in WBG-projects strengthens the argument that OPs are inadequate and require strengthening and that the WBG in general needs to better address human rights issues throughout its operations. While cases may not be brought against the Bank directly – it enjoys immunity from domestic legal action – they may nonetheless be brought against the government in relation to the same Bank-financed project and therefore decisions may apply by association to the Bank as well. The IFC is not necessarily immune and can be sued in countries where it maintains a country office. IFC clients may also be sued in domestic venues as may host governments for failure to protect indigenous peoples from violations perpetrated by corporations. In either case, where applicable, international complaints may then be filed once domestic remedies have been exhausted.

C. Programmatic level

Addressing issues at the programmatic level is a great deal more complicated than it is at either the policy or project levels. This is especially the case as many programmatic loans are not well publicized, if at all, and are not subject to the safeguard policies applying to indigenous peoples including the participation requirements set out therein. The main suggestion with regard to programmatic lending is to try and identify these loans and raise concerns before they are approved or otherwise at the earliest stage possible and to lobby both the government and the Bank to ensure that indigenous peoples are involved in decision making.

5

A Framework for Advocacy in Support of Indigenous Peoples' Visions, Perspectives and Strategies for Self-Determining Development

Victoria Tauli-Corpuz

I. Introduction

The United Nations Permanent Forum on Indigenous Issues urges States, the United Nations (UN) system and other intergovernmental organizations to "support the efforts of indigenous peoples to build, articulate and implement their visions of and strategies for development."[1] In this light, the establishment of appropriate policy and institutional frameworks was identified as an important component of such efforts. Likewise, a review of good development practices of projects in support of indigenous peoples came up with a similar recommendation.[2] The review noted that supporting specific projects for indigenous peoples that reinforce development as determined by them is a necessary but insufficient measure.[3] It is crucial to complement these projects with advocacy work from the local to the global levels to foster greater understanding and support for indigenous peoples' self-determining development.

The development model of international financial institutions, the UN system and bilateral and multilateral donors is generally regarded by indigenous peoples as more of a problem than a solution. This is mainly because this development model ignores and undermines indigenous peoples' natural resource management systems, and indigenous economies and traditional livelihoods that have sustained them through generations. Furthermore, they are not consulted nor involved in making decisions on development projects brought to their communities. At worst, violations of their basic human rights take place in the development process and this phenomenon has been labelled by them as "development aggression". Even new platforms, such as the Millennium Development Goals (MDGs) and Poverty Reduction Strategy Papers (PRSPs) fail to take indigenous peoples' rights and issues into account.[4]

The challenge, therefore, is to bring about development with a strong social and cultural dimension, which promotes respect for the basic human rights of indigenous peoples and which integrates their own development visions. The Inter-Agency Support Group (IASG) in their statement on indigenous peoples and the MDGs said that:

> the main challenge is to interpret and qualify the Millennium Development Goals as related to the rights and priorities of indigenous peoples in a way that is relevant and attributes to indigenous peoples a sense of ownership in the process, and to articulate the Millennium Development Goals within the framework of international human rights standards.[5]

---

[1] See Paragraph 12 of the UN Permanent Forum on Indigenous Issues Report on Fourth Session (16-27 May 2005), E/2005/43 and E/C.19/2005/9. p. 4.

[2] This refers to a review of some projects funded by the International Fund for Agricultural Development that were implemented in indigenous peoples' territories in Brazil, Peru, Bolivia and Northeast India.

[3] It was seen that lessons learned from implementing specific projects were not used in a systematic manner to bring about changes in government policies on development work done among indigenous peoples. The case studies will be made available soon on the website of the Permanent Forum.

[4] This is a conclusion that emerged from analysis of some MDG national reports and Country PRSPs, which were done by the International Labour Organization (ILO) and the Secretariat of the Permanent Forum on Indigenous Issues.

[5] See UN E/C.19/2005/2. Report of Inter-Agency Support Group on Indigenous Issues on its 2004 Session (14 Feb. 2004). p. 20.

5

While the MDGs are just a subset of a broader development framework, this can provide the springboard upon which indigenous peoples' development can be further reinforced and debated.

Within the past two decades there have been positive developments in the areas of standard-setting on indigenous peoples' rights and the formulation of policies by intergovernmental bodies, international financial institutions and bilateral donors on indigenous peoples development.[6] This includes existing legally binding international standards on indigenous peoples rights that are stated in ILO Convention 107 and ILO Convention No. 169[7] and the emerging standard which is the Draft Declaration on the Rights of Indigenous Peoples. It also includes policies on indigenous peoples' development which came out from the World Bank, donor agencies and UN programmes like the UNDP.

In May 2003 the Interagency Workshop on the Human Rights-based Approach came up with a document entitled "The Human Rights Based Approach to Development Cooperation: Towards a Common Understanding Among UN Agencies". Since the international financial institutions (IFIs) and the donor community are key players in development work among indigenous peoples, it is the hope of indigenous peoples that these entities will use the human rights-based approach as a guiding framework in their development work. The World Bank is a specialized UN Agency but the other IFIs and bilateral donors are not. So it cannot be assumed that these bodies are part of this common understanding. Nevertheless, as this is an approach which resonates significantly with indigenous peoples' own views and perspectives on development, the IFIs and bilateral donors should endeavour to use this also as their guiding framework.

II. Background

Participants at the IASG on Indigenous Issues meeting in 2004 expressed concern that:

> *the effort to meet the targets laid down for the achievement of the Millennium Development Goals could in fact have harmful effects on indigenous and tribal peoples, such as the acceleration of the loss of the lands and natural resources on which indigenous peoples' livelihoods have traditionally depended or the displacement of indigenous peoples from those lands.*[8]

---

[6] Some policies of intergovernmental organizations and international financial institutions policies include the following: the UNDP Policy of Engagement with Indigenous Peoples (2001), the World Bank OP 4.10 on Indigenous Peoples which superseded the OD 4.20, the Asian Development Bank Policy on Indigenous Peoples, the Inter-American Development Bank Draft Strategic Framework for Indigenous Development, European Union 1998 Council Resolution in Support of Indigenous Peoples, etc. Examples of policies of bilateral donors are as follows: Strategy for Danish Support to Indigenous Peoples (1994), Netherlands: National Advisory Council for Development Cooperation's Recommendation on Indigenous Peoples (1993), Germany: Policy for Development Cooperation for Indigenous Peoples in Latin America (1996), United Kingdom: Guidance on Ethnicity, Ethnic Minorities and Indigenous Peoples (1995), Spain: Strategy for Co-operation with Indigenous Peoples in Latin America (1997), Spanish Strategy for Co-operation with Indigenous Peoples (2005).

[7] ILO Convention No. 169 has been ratified by 17 States as of 2005. These are Mexico, Denmark, Ecuador, Fiji, Norway, Venezuela, Argentina, Costa Rica, Colombia, Honduras, Peru, The Netherlands, Guatemala, Bolivia, Dominica, Paraguay, Brazil and Panama.

[8] See Annex II *"Statement adopted by the Inter-Agency Support Group on Indigenous Issues regarding indigenous peoples and the Millennium Development Goals,"* E/C.19/2005/2. p.11.

5

As the situation of indigenous peoples is often not reflected in statistics or is hidden by national averages, the IASG further stated that while national indicators may show some progress in the achievement of the MDGs, the negative impacts on indigenous peoples may remain invisible.

Poverty studies on indigenous peoples done by IFIs and other intergovernmental organizations during the past two decades confirm that most poverty maps still coincide with indigenous territories. Indigenous peoples compose around 5 percent of the world's population but represent 15 percent of the world's poor. In many countries they are the poorest of the poor. Studies conducted in several countries in Latin America, Africa and Asia show that most indigenous peoples are in situations of pervasive, chronic and severe poverty. The most recent World Bank study, presented during the Fourth Session of the UN Permanent Forum, was on the indigenous poverty situation in five Latin American countries.[9] It looked at the changes in the poverty situation of indigenous peoples during the International Decade of the World's Indigenous People (1994-2004). Some of the study's conclusions are as follows:

- Few gains were made in income poverty reduction among indigenous peoples during the Indigenous Peoples' Decade (1994-2004);

- Indigenous peoples recover more slowly from economic crisis.[10] A policy environment that successfully brings about poverty reduction for the population at large may not equally benefit indigenous peoples;

- The indigenous poverty gap is deeper and shrank more slowly over the 1990s;

- Being indigenous increases an individual's probability of being poor and this relationship was about the same at the beginning and at the close of the Decade;

- Education outcomes are substantially worse for indigenous peoples, indicative of problems in education quality;

- There is systemic evidence of worse health conditions among indigenous peoples. Indigenous women and children continue to have lesser access to basic health services; therefore, major differences in indigenous and non-indigenous health indicators persist.

While these conclusions were reached from studies in Latin America, similar trends can be gleaned from other studies such as the one made by the International Labour Organization (ILO).[11] The ILO did an ethnic audit of the PRSPs of 14 countries.[12] One conclusion reached is that "most of the PRSPs recognize that poverty is widespread and persistent among indigenous and tribal peoples or in those areas prevalently occupied by them." This study also shows that the serious lack of reliable, up-to-date statistics and disaggregated data is

---

[9] See Gillete Hall and Harry Anthony Patrinos (2005), *Indigenous Peoples, Poverty and Human Development in Latin America: 1994-2004.* Unpublished manuscript. The countries included in the study were Bolivia, Ecuador, Guatemala, Mexico and Peru.

[10] This is confirmed by findings of the International Fund on Agricultural Development in studies done in the aftermath of the Asian economic crisis and also after the tsunami.

[11] See Manuela Tomei (2005). *Indigenous and Tribal Peoples: An Ethnic Audit of Selected Poverty Reduction Strategy Papers.* ILO, Geneva.

[12] The countries whose PRSPs were reviewed were Bangladesh, Bolivia, Cambodia, Guyana, Honduras, Kenya, Lao PDR, Nepal, Nicaragua, Pakistan, Sri Lanka, Tanzania, Viet Nam and Zambia.

a major factor in the disjuncture between poverty diagnostics and poverty-reduction strategies addressing indigenous peoples. A similar observation was presented by the IASG. It stated:

> A review of the Millennium Development Goal progress reports in countries that have significant populations of indigenous peoples reveals that few are undertaking the effort needed to provide specific information and disaggregated data on the poverty of indigenous peoples.[13]

Clearly, there is a need to undertake similar poverty studies among indigenous peoples in other regions. Future studies, however, should go deeper into identifying the structural causes of indigenous poverty, develop appropriate indicators and come up with relevant recommendations for future action. It is increasingly recognized that indigenous peoples remain poor, not because they do not have the resources or knowledge to change their situation, but because they have been denied of their rights to have control and access to their resources and protection of their traditional knowledge.

The IASG aptly summarized this point:

> As the result of various historical processes, indigenous peoples have often been excluded from political participation in the States in which they live and their rights to land and resources are seldom recognized. Indigenous peoples also suffer disproportionately from human rights abuses and the effects of conflict. As noted in the report of the United Nations Special Rapporteur on the situation of human rights and fundamental freedoms of indigenous peoples (A/59/258), "(i) indigenous peoples the world over are usually among the most marginalized and dispossessed sectors of society, because they suffer discrimination and face prejudices that are often perpetuated within societies" (para. 10).[14]

Discrimination is the lot of most indigenous peoples and this is a major cause of their poverty. They are subjected to discrimination by state authorities and also by the elite and dominant populations. This is more felt by the poor, however, as poverty exacerbates discrimination.

The reports of the UN Special Rapporteur on the Situation of Human Rights and Fundamental Freedoms of Indigenous People confirm the appalling poverty situation of indigenous peoples, which is closely interlinked with the continuing violations of their basic human rights. In his report presented to the General Assembly in September 2005 the Rapporteur concluded:

> ...this complex panorama of persistent poverty is rooted in the conditions of destitution, discrimination and structural inequality ...and such multidimensional poverty cannot be overcome through a piecemeal approach; rather, it requires comprehensive public policies, which most States and multinational agencies unfortunately have not yet developed for indigenous peoples.[15]

5

---

[13] See "Technical Position Paper prepared by the Inter-Agency Support Group on Indigenous Issues on the Millennium Development Goals and Indigenous Peoples," Annex III of UN E/C.19/2005/2.

[14] Ibid. p. 15, paragraph 6.

[15] See United Nations General Assembly Document A/60/358, 16 September 2005, The Situation of Human Rights and Fundamental Freedoms of Indigenous People. p. 10.

In some areas where indigenous peoples are vigorously asserting their rights, conflict situations emerge. Some of these conflicts are intractable and remain unresolved. Development assistance has had both positive and negative contributions in the resolution or exacerbation of such conflicts. There are conflicts in indigenous territories that have been ended through political settlements, but post-conflict programmes have not yet adequately addressed the reasons why such conflicts came about in the first place. Effective mechanisms that can provide redress for the injustice and human rights violations committed against indigenous peoples in the name of national development are not yet in place. The realization of human rights requires recognition of conflicts between competing rights and the design of mechanisms for negotiation and conflict-resolution.

It is important to acknowledge that there are various efforts on the part of intergovernmental organizations, NGOs and some governments to support self-determining development priorities of indigenous peoples. Some even helped set up mechanisms for negotiating conflicts between competing rights. However, there are not enough of these to significantly change the poverty situations of indigenous peoples. More widespread replication of such experiences within countries is very much needed so that these will not remain as isolated or exceptional cases. More effective communication strategies should also be implemented so that such experiences and the lessons learned can be shared more widely.

It is within this context the advocacy framework has been developed. This framework is in support of indigenous peoples' visions, strategies and perspectives on development. It draws substantially from the *Technical position paper prepared by the Inter-Agency Support Group on Indigenous Issues on the Millennium Development Goals and indigenous peoples*,[16] which was submitted during the Fourth Session of the UN Permanent Forum on Indigenous Issues. The ideas presented here, which include proposed areas of work, are drawn from various discussions with indigenous peoples and with other development actors from intergovernmental bodies and NGOs. An Annex which further elaborates on the points raised in the main paper is included.

III. Objective and basic underlying principles

Objective:

- **To advocate for development that reflects indigenous peoples' own vision, perspectives and strategies of self-determining development within the framework of respect for their basic human rights and fundamental freedoms and to effectively monitor this using indicators that are sensitive and relevant to their specific conditions.**

The basic normative framework upon which an advocacy for indigenous peoples' rights and development is grounded upon is international human rights law as enshrined in the Universal Declaration on Human Rights and the International Covenants on Civil and

---

[16] See Annex III of E/C.19/2005/2.

Political Rights and on Economic, Social and Cultural Rights as well as other core human rights treaties.[17] States which ratified the core human rights instruments are legally bound to respect, protect, promote, and work towards the realization of these. The ILO Convention No. 169 and the UN Draft Declaration on the Rights of Indigenous Peoples[18], decisions of treaty bodies, Declarations and Plans of Actions of World Conferences and Summits (e.g. Agenda 21, Vienna Declaration and Plan of Action, Johannesburg Declaration, Beijing Plan of Action, etc.) form part of this normative framework.

The key principles which underpin such a framework are the following:

1. Human rights-based approach to development

The basic premise of this approach is that development should enable people to live in dignity and to attain the highest standards of humanity guaranteed by international human rights law. A statement of UN Agencies on how they understand the Human Rights-Based Approach to Development Cooperation[19] provides, among other points, that:

■ All programmes of development cooperation, policies and technical assistance should further the realization of human rights as laid down in the Universal Declaration of Human Rights and other international human rights instruments.

■ Human rights standards contained in, and principles derived from, the Universal Declaration of Human Rights and other international human rights instruments guide all development cooperation and programming in all sectors and in all phases of the programming process.

■ Development cooperation contributes to the development of the capacities of 'duty bearers' to meet their obligations and of 'rights-holders' to claim their rights.

2. Non-discrimination and equality

The fundamental principles of international human rights law are equality and non-discrimination. This explicitly prohibits discrimination based on race, colour, language, religion, political or other opinion, national or social origin, property, birth or other status.[20] All individuals are equal as human beings and by virtue of the inherent dignity of each human person.

5

---

[17] This includes the International Convention on the Elimination of all Forms of Racial Discrimination, 1965; Convention on the Elimination of all Forms of Discrimination Against Women, l979; Convention on the Rights of the Child, 1989; International Convention on the Protection of the Rights of all Migrant Workers and Members of their Families, l990; among others.

[18] While the UN Draft Declaration on Indigenous Peoples Rights still remain as a Draft and, therefore, does not have the same status as the other Conventions, it is regarded as an emerging standard on the rights of indigenous peoples and it has been cited and used as a basis for the formulation of existing intergovernmental policies and national laws (e.g. 1997 Indigenous Peoples Rights Act of the Philippines).

[19] See "The Human Rights Based Approach to Development Cooperation: Towards a Common Understanding Among UN Agencies." Available at www.undp.org/governance/dochurist/031616/CommonUnderstanding.doc

[20] Article 3 of the Universal Declaration of Human Rights.

3. Respect for individual and collective rights

Indigenous peoples possess collective rights that are indispensable for their existence, well-being and holistic development as peoples. These include the right to self-determination, right to territories, lands and resources, and right to culture, among others. Individual rights of indigenous persons as enshrined in international human rights law should likewise be respected.

4. Self-determination

The right to self-determination is a fundamental right of all peoples, including indigenous peoples. It is the basis for the broader recognition of their right to have control over their institutions, territories, resources, and cultures without external domination or interference; their right to freely pursue their own economic, social and cultural development and to establish their relationship with the dominant society and the State on the basis of consent.[21]

5. Empowerment

The international normative framework empowers indigenous peoples by granting them rights; thus, it is imperative to make them aware of their rights. It also means enhancing the capabilities of indigenous women and men to assert their rights and claim their entitlements in a democratic and equitable manner. The human rights-based development approach is aimed at the empowerment of people and therefore it rejects the welfare or charity approach. Creating spaces and mechanisms which allow for their full and effective participation in decision-making is a key component.

6. Free, prior and informed consent

The principle of free, prior and informed consent of indigenous peoples to development projects and plans affecting them, is emerging as a standard to be applied in protecting and promoting their rights in the development process.[22] Mechanisms should be established which ensure that indigenous peoples are able to give their free, prior and informed consent to activities affecting them, using processes that take into account their own methods of consultation and decision-making.

7. Gender equality

Ensuring equality between genders is crucial for indigenous development. Particular attention has to be given to gender differences and inequalities. Gender equality ensures that the rights and voices of women and men are heard and that differentiated approaches and responses are adopted to address gender discrimination and inequalities. Gender equality should be promoted as a basic norm in the political, social and economic fields.

---

[21] This right is contained in common Article 1 of the International Covenant on Civil and Political Rights and the International Covenant on Economic, Social and Cultural Rights as well as Article 3 of the UN Draft Declaration on the Rights of Indigenous Peoples.

[22] Article 7 (1) of the ILO Convention No. 169 recognizes that indigenous peoples "shall have the right to decide their own priorities for the process of development as it affects their lives, beliefs, institutions and spiritual well-being and the lands they occupy or otherwise use, and to exercise control, to the extent possible, over their own economic, social and cultural development. In addition, they shall participate in the formulation, implementation and evaluation of plans and programmes for national and regional development which may affect them directly."

8. Accountability and establishing legal obligations and duties on States

States and other duty-bearers are answerable for the observance of human rights and they have to comply with the legal norms and standards enshrined in human rights instruments. When they fail to do so, aggrieved rights-holders are entitled to institute proceedings for appropriate redress before a competent court or other adjudicators in accordance with the rules and procedures provided by law.[23]

9. Respect for cultural diversity, cultural identity and indigenous knowledge

An advocacy framework for development, which will have relevance for indigenous peoples, has to have strong cultural underpinnings. It should respect their distinct cultural identities and ensure their control over their own diverse economic, political and socio-cultural systems. Indigenous knowledge systems, which evolved through generations and which are used for the common good, should be protected and developed to prevent appropriation and commercialization by others without indigenous peoples' free, prior and informed consent.

10. Sustainability

The balance between economic, social and environment objectives should guide any development process related to indigenous peoples.

IV. Capacity-building and communication strategies

Advocacy is understood as a continuous process of influencing or changing policies, frameworks, laws, and programmes of institutions, groups and individuals who are in positions of power, towards the betterment of affected peoples. In this case, we are talking about a framework for advocacy that will lead to a better understanding, respect and support of indigenous peoples' perspectives and strategies for self-determining development. It also involves collecting and packaging information into a persuasive case and communicating these to decision-makers and potential supporters, including the general public. This means developing and effectively using interpersonal relationships and the media which includes modern information and communication technologies.

Each advocacy actor should give consideration to adopting a series of capacity-building and communications strategies, capitalizing on the opportunities offered by the Second International Decade of the World's Indigenous People and the Millennium Declaration, including the MDGs. These can be along the following lines:

1. **Build awareness and undertake sensitization activities for high-officials, senior management and staff of key bodies involved in development work, such as international financial institutions, the UN system and other multilateral bodies.**

---

[23] Ibid.

It is fundamental to build awareness on the rights and situation of indigenous peoples among high officials, senior management and staff of these bodies from the country level to the international level. This sensitization process can also lead to a better understanding of indigenous peoples' issues, perspectives and strategies on development, in general, and their critiques and recommendations on the MDGs, in particular. Forms and methods of sensitization vary depending on the roles and responsibilities of these persons. With high officials and senior management experts, the Permanent Forum can seek audiences with them to discuss such issues. For staff directly dealing with indigenous peoples, it is important to raise their awareness on indigenous peoples' rights and international human rights law; existing policies and laws on indigenous peoples on the national level; recommendations and relevant documents of the UN Permanent Forum on Indigenous Issues, the Working Group on Indigenous Populations and reports of the Special Rapporteur on the situation of human rights and fundamental freedoms of indigenous people, as well as other existing policies on indigenous peoples of multilateral and bilateral organizations.

It is important to popularize the document "The Human Rights-Based Approach to Development Cooperation: Towards a Common Understanding among UN Agencies" so that it will be better internalized. The operationalization of this approach remains the biggest challenge. Personnel of aforementioned institutions should work in close partnership with indigenous peoples to operationalize the human rights-based approach to indigenous peoples' development. Mechanisms can be created for sustained dialogues and discussions between these development actors and indigenous peoples so more concrete steps can be taken towards better integration of indigenous peoples' perspectives and strategies on development

2. **Analyse and assess existing institutional development frameworks, policies, instruments, programmes and projects affecting indigenous peoples.**

Personnel of IFIs and IASG members can make an analysis of their institution's frameworks, policies, programmes and projects to see how these are consistent or contradictory to indigenous peoples' visions, perspectives and strategies on development. They can also review and evaluate their existing projects and programmes in indigenous peoples' communities to gather good practices and lessons learned. Recommendations on how to upscale good practices and how to advocate for relevant changes in existing frameworks, policies, programmes and projects can be evolved and implemented. Sharing of analysis and studies between them can be facilitated and common recommendations on what can be done to make frameworks, policies, programmes and projects more supportive of indigenous peoples can be evolved. The key principles identified in this document can be used as guides in this endeavour.

For agencies with specific policies on indigenous peoples, reviews and evaluations done on the monitoring, implementation or revision of these policies can also be shared and discussed. Results of these analyses and studies can be presented in relevant processes of the agencies, i.e. Governing Council meetings, Executive Committee meetings, Inter-agency processes, Permanent Forum on Indigenous Issues, etc. These results can also be the basis for advocating changes in the development frameworks, policies, programmes and projects to be more relevant and appropriate for indigenous peoples or for creating new policies and programmes.

3. **Establish partnerships with indigenous peoples' organizations, experts, NGOs and bilateral donors for mutual support in advocacy work.**

For the two components above, it is important to work in partnership with indigenous peoples' organizations and experts, NGOs, other agencies, bilateral donors and States. Awareness-building and analytical evaluations can be done jointly with the various actors. Effort should be exerted to ensure that indigenous peoples are effectively participating in these processes. Partnership-building includes enhancing the capacities of indigenous peoples to do advocacy work themselves. This includes indigenous people developing an understanding of the nature, mechanisms and processes of the IFIs, the UN system and the donor community and providing them with training, toolkits, etc. so that they can effectively lobby governments and intergovernmental bodies. This also means openly sharing with them the lessons learned and good practices in development work in indigenous territories and involving them directly in reviews and evaluations of policies, programmes and projects.

4. **Provide appropriate technical assistance and capacity-building activities to member states.**

One of the primary roles of the IFIs and IASG members is to support their member states through technical assistance, capacity building and funding (loans or grants). They can consider how this support could be geared towards increasing their members' capacities to comply with their legal and moral obligations to international human rights standards and environmental laws. This means increasing their capacities to promote and respect the basic rights and fundamental freedoms of indigenous peoples and to understand and support indigenous peoples' development perspectives and priorities. This also means supporting them to amend or redesign existing laws, frameworks, policies, programmes and projects that are discriminatory to indigenous people; or helping to establish laws, policies or programmes that promote indigenous peoples' rights and priorities for development. It can also mean strengthening the capacities of national machinery responsible for human rights, indigenous peoples' rights, women and children's rights, among others, to be more effective in implementing their mandates. The review of MDG implementation, poverty reduction strategies, Common Country Assessments/UN Development Assistance Framework to see how these have integrated indigenous peoples' concerns is another area where IFIs and IASG members can help governments and indigenous peoples.

5. **Develop training modules and toolkits and undertake training activities on indigenous peoples' rights, perspectives and strategies on self-determining development and how to use existing policies on indigenous peoples.**

To be able to effectively address the points raised above, it is important that the IFIs, bilateral and multilateral donors and IASG members share with each other the policies, guidebooks, toolkits or training materials and modules that they have developed. Training activities among IFI staff, UN staff, government bureaucrats, NGOs and even indigenous peoples can be undertaken using existing modules and toolkits. Programmes like HURIST (Human Rights Strengthening (a joint programme between UNDP and OHCHR)), ILO training programmes for its staff, can be replicated by other agencies. The development and use of guidebooks by the IFIs on how to implement their policies on indigenous peoples should be done as soon as possible. Both indigenous peoples and governments should be familiarized with these policies, toolkits and guidebooks.

5

6. **Enhance and institutionalize support for indigenous peoples' priorities and strategies on self-determining development.**

IFIs, bilateral and multilateral donors and UN agencies may further strengthen, institutionalize and systematize their support for indigenous peoples through the enhancement of support for focal points on indigenous issues. Mechanisms for coordination on indigenous issues within an institution or agency and in between these entities, and existing units solely addressing indigenous peoples' issues (i.e. Permanent Forum on Indigenous Issues, Indigenous Peoples' Team in the OHCHR, Indigenous Team in the Convention on Biological Diversity, etc.) should also be given more support in terms of personnel and funds. Those agencies that do not have such mechanisms are encouraged to set these up as soon as possible.

The Inter-Agency Support Group on Indigenous Issues is a very innovative development. So far, its operations have been very important for indigenous peoples. The members of the IASG should explore further how they can implement the recommendations arising out of the Permanent Forum that specifically addressed indigenous peoples. Further discussions should be undertaken with Permanent Forum members on the constraints and potentials in implementing these recommendations. Communication plans on the work of each agency on indigenous issues, as well as on the work of the IASG, should be developed. The IASG, together with the Permanent Forum members and governments, can explore further how to advocate effectively, giving more attention to indigenous peoples' issues at the Economic and Social Council and at the General Assembly. The IASG members can also undertake the dissemination of reports of agencies dealing with indigenous peoples in a more systematic and wide-scale fashion. The IASG has expanded its membership to include not only UN bodies, organizations and programmes but also multilateral bodies, such as the European Commission and other funding mechanisms like the Indigenous Fund of Latin America. More IFIs, in addition to the World Bank, should also be invited to become part of this IASG.

7. **Support efforts of indigenous peoples to further elaborate their vision, framework and strategies for self-determining development.**

While there are scattered efforts by indigenous peoples, NGOs and some intergovernmental agencies to articulate and put into writing indigenous peoples' visions and strategies on development, there has not been an organized effort to bring these efforts together and to come up with a consolidated framework. The IFIs, bilateral and multilateral donors and the IASG can support the efforts of indigenous peoples to do this.

8. **Develop effective communication strategies.**

It is important to effectively communicate the work of each agency on indigenous issues to their own decision-makers and also to the general public. Opportunities to present these in appropriate processes and bodies, such as the meetings of the Economic and Social Council and the General Assembly, Governing Council or Executive Board meetings, among others, should be maximized. Focal persons on indigenous issues should be appointed where they do not exist. To be more efficient in their work, which includes implementation of communication plans, the focal persons should not be unduly burdened with other tasks. Communication plans can include the organization of exhibits, panels or roundtable discussions where examples of indigenous peoples' development visions, strategies and initiatives are discussed and debated with others. The facilitation of exposure trips of government officials to areas where there are good practices on indigenous peoples' development can also be undertaken. Proper documentation of such good practices that make use of multimedia can be done so that these can be communicated more widely.

V. Conclusions

This framework for advocacy is a work in progress. It is meant to initiate discussion and debate on the challenges and opportunities in advocating for indigenous peoples' rights and development. It recognizes the critical role of the IFIs, the bilateral and multilateral donors and the UN system in such advocacy efforts. It underscores the need to ensure the full and effective participation of indigenous peoples not only in doing advocacy work but in decision-making processes on policies, programmes and projects which affect them.

Advocacy work for indigenous peoples' development with governments, intergovernmental bodies, and non-government actors has to be guided by the human rights-based approach. Much more work has to be done to further elaborate and effectively implement this approach for indigenous peoples. This challenge has to be seriously addressed. It is hoped that when the Second Decade of the World's Indigenous Peoples ends in 2015, significant positive impacts in terms of changing the face of indigenous peoples' poverty and reinforcement of their self-determining economic, social, cultural and political development are achieved.

5

CHAPTER 5 ANNEX: Further elaboration of key areas of work

Note – this is a preliminary indicative list. Some parts are more developed than others. It is a work in progress, so more suggestions for improvement are welcome.

1. **Elaborate and operationalize the human rights-based approach for indigenous peoples' self-determining development.**

Since the adoption of the human rights-based approach in 1999 (CCA/UNDAF)[24] there has been an increasing recognition that it has to be applied. However, its implementation and operationalization in relation to indigenous peoples is not happening in any significant manner. This is an approach and a framework that speaks of the realities and aspirations of indigenous peoples. It is imperative, therefore, to develop and implement a human rights-based approach specifically for indigenous peoples' development. This can be done jointly by the IFIs, bilateral and multilateral donor bodies and the UN system, states and indigenous peoples. The human-rights based approach cannot be fully implemented unless it includes the understanding of indigenous peoples' self-determining development. Some activities which can be undertaken are as follows:

1.1. Support for indigenous peoples to make reports on their actual experiences with respect to the enjoyment and denial of their human rights and fundamental freedoms within a given state, using as a yardstick the international human rights norms and standards.

1.2. Identification of steps that States are obliged to take, in order to comply with their legal obligations under international law, and with their political commitments in international conferences.

1.3. Technical assistance for governments to build their capacities and political will in meeting their obligations.

1.4. Assistance for indigenous organizations and communities to raise their own awareness on their fundamental human rights; to build their capacity to act together to assert these rights; to recognize and act upon the policies, laws and practices of government and international institutions that play a role in their impoverishment; and to get states to comply with their obligations.

1.5. Support efforts towards the early adoption of a United Nations Declaration on the Rights of Indigenous Peoples as this is a crucial part of the normative framework for a human rights-based development approach for them.

1.6. Develop a consolidated document on "The human rights-based approach to development and indigenous peoples". This can be developed by the Permanent Forum jointly with indigenous peoples and government experts, IFIs, bilateral and multilateral donors and the Inter-Agency Support Group.

1.7. Undertake case studies of good practices of IFIs and UN agencies in terms of operationalizing the human rights-based approach for indigenous peoples.

1.8. Analyse various existing development frameworks and approaches (i.e. sustainable livelihoods approach, people-centred development approaches, human rights-based approach to development, gender approach, development with identity, development with culture, life projects, etc.). Review policies of donor agencies and intergovernmental bodies (i.e. Strategy for Danish Support to Indigenous Peoples, UNDP Policy of Engagement with Indigenous Peoples, WB OD 4.10, ADB Policy on Indigenous Peoples, etc.). Strengthen the good elements that can reinforce indigenous peoples' self-determining development and reform the weak or negative parts.

1.9. Undertake participatory processes with representatives of indigenous organizations, governments and intergovernmental bodies to discuss how to further support self-determining development of indigenous peoples.

---

[24] CCA/UNDAF and Common Understanding of HRBA to Development Cooperation.

2. Collect disaggregated data on indigenous peoples and develop indicators sensitive to the situation of indigenous peoples.

The lack of disaggregated data based on ethnicity precludes an accurate assessment of where indigenous peoples are, who and how many they are, what their living conditions are, situations of poverty, etc. The existence of such information will strengthen cases for introducing programmes and policy reforms in the various systems and processes of governments, intergovernmental bodies, and even NGOs. This includes reforms in health and education systems, economic production models, natural resources and environmental management, among others, to be more appropriate and responsive to indigenous peoples' issues and aspirations. Disaggregated statistical data is a tool for promoting relevant actions and programmes. Conversely, the lack of data by ethnicity perpetuates the invisibility of indigenous peoples and inequities within national societies. The development of indicators that are relevant and sensitive to indigenous peoples' perspectives and realities is an integral part of the data disaggregation project. Ensure indigenous peoples' participation in the elaboration and execution of development activities.

Some proposed activities:

2.1. Strengthening national capacities in the area of data collection and disaggregation. Government agencies doing statistical surveys should be equipped to undertake disaggregated data collection to ensure that indigenous peoples will be made visible in national statistics. This baseline data will be needed in the monitoring of the impact of programmes and policies on them. Data collection and disaggregation must be undertaken with the full participation of indigenous peoples, using indigenous languages and employing indigenous facilitators and enumerators. This means involvement of indigenous experts and organizations in all phases of statistical work from: a) development of data collection instruments, b) data collection, c) tabulation, d) analysis and e) dissemination.

2.2. Disaggregation based on ethnicity should be integrated into the data generation activities undertaken by specific government ministries or departments such as those in health, education, agriculture, labour, women, children, housing, etc.

2.3. The development of indigenous-sensitive indicators is an important component of data disaggregation. This is crucial for benchmarking, impact assessment, poverty studies, etc. and in ensuring respect for the diversity of concepts and perceptions of poverty, well-being, quality of life as well as the realization of indigenous peoples' basic economic, social and cultural rights.

3. Carry out impact assessment studies and reviews of existing policies, frameworks, strategies, programmes and policies that affect indigenous peoples.

This includes comprehensive assessments of impacts on indigenous peoples of national or institutional frameworks and policies on development, poverty alleviation and social sector programmes. Develop and use indigenous peoples' expertise in conducting such assessments. Encourage all development actors to formulate and implement policies on indigenous peoples or to review and strengthen their existing policies.

Some proposed activities are the following:

3.1. Undertake assessments of the social, human rights and environmental impacts of existing frameworks, policies and programmes of governments , intergovernmental agencies and institutions as these relate to the protection or denial of their basic rights to self-determination, rights to land, territories and resources, cultural rights, among others. This can include comprehensive assessments of impacts on indigenous peoples of national or institutional frameworks and policies on development, poverty alleviation, social sector programmes, etc.

3.2. Conduct impact assessments of poverty reduction, frameworks and strategies, in general, and Poverty Reduction Strategy Papers (PRSPs), in particular, to see how these either alleviate or exacerbate indigenous peoples' poverty situations.

5

3.3. A review of the implementation of the Millennium Declaration and the Millennium Development Goals from the perspective of indigenous peoples should also be undertaken. This can lead to the generation of parallel country reports on "Millennium Development Goals and Indigenous Peoples", which could be presented to the fifth session of the Permanent Forum on Indigenous Issues.

3.4. Conduct impact assessments of global, regional and bilateral rules on trade, investment and finance as they affect indigenous peoples. Increasing evidence shows that the liberalization of trade, finance and investments has direct effects on indigenous peoples. Case studies in specific countries could be done to show what these impacts are, including specific recommendations on how these should be addressed.

4. Identify and increase allocation of resources for indigenous peoples' development. Carry out budget analysis and promote participatory budgeting processes for indigenous peoples.

Budget analysis is a tool that can be used to understand and advocate for better resource allocation for indigenous peoples. Such analysis can also help in assessing needs and establishing benchmarks in sectoral areas of concern to indigenous peoples, as well as directly linking these to the MDGs. The efforts and experience of the UN system and other development actors in mainstreaming gender in budgets can serve as a useful tool for indigenous related budgeting. Best practices of participatory budgeting can be used to enhance indigenous peoples' participation. It is necessary to assist governments and parliaments in using participatory budgeting processes at all levels. This also applies to intergovernmental organizations.

Some proposed activities are the following:

4.1. Undertake budget analysis in some countries to identify the level of resource allocations targeted for indigenous peoples and in which areas these are used.

4.2. Develop further the concept of indigenous budgeting, using gender budgeting as a model, and evolve and disseminate this as a tool.

5. Reinforce respect and protection of indigenous peoples' rights over their lands, territories and resources.

5.1. Analyse in depth existing laws, policies, programmes and projects on lands and natural resource management (water, forests, biodiversity, etc.) to see how these conflict with or reinforce indigenous peoples' world views, customary laws and practices on natural resource management.

5.2. Use existing studies on indigenous land tenure systems and customary laws on land as a basis to further develop or reinforce relevant policies and programs which ensure control and access of indigenous peoples to their lands and territories.

5.3. Undertake research on good practices of programmes and projects of governments, intergovernmental agencies, NGOs, indigenous organizations and communities, which have strengthened the protection and respect of indigenous peoples' rights to lands, territories and resources.

5.4. Gather and document agreements, treaties, contracts signed between indigenous peoples and states or the private sector on land claims, access and benefit-sharing, free, prior and informed consent, etc. and put these on a database which can be accessed and used by those who need them.

5.5. Learn lessons from policies, programmes and projects strengthening indigenous peoples' natural resource management practices and use these to formulate more comprehensive and indigenous-sensitive natural resource management policies, programmes and projects.

5

6. Protect indigenous peoples' traditional livelihood and economic systems. Encourage the development of indigenous peoples' traditional economy and ensure food security.

The acceleration of the process of alienation, privatization and commercialization of indigenous peoples' resources (including forests, lands, waters, sub-surface resources, biogenetic resources and medicinal plants) due to internal and external actors has considerably eroded the livelihood systems of indigenous peoples. In order for governments to reach the MDGs in an equitable and fair manner, systematic and concerted efforts are required to restore and enhance these systems. In the past, other interests drove innovations in indigenous peoples' communities. It is time to support indigenous peoples' innovations and to give them the say on what innovations and technologies should be developed in their communities.

7. Protect and develop indigenous knowledge systems.

Indigenous knowledge systems are integral to indigenous cultures, including indigenous economies. Such systems, which were developed over generation, also define indigenous peoples' identities and their management of biodiversity. These systems are valuable for humankind, yet, they are now under threat by commercial interests or other policies that deeply affect indigenous cultures and their expressions. Assisting in the protection and development of traditional knowledge, therefore, is a contribution to sustainable human development of indigenous peoples and of society, as a whole.

8. Reinforce indigenous health systems and practices and develop holistic, appropriate, accessible and affordable health services for indigenous peoples.

Providing health care to indigenous peoples, at least on an equal basis as the rest of the population, is a minimum requirement. However, to go beyond this, it is important that indigenous health systems and practices be considered when developing health care delivery systems among them.

9. Revitalize, strengthen and develop indigenous teaching and learning institutions and systems and work towards reforming public and private education systems at all levels.

The enhancement and revitalization of indigenous learning systems is a necessity for the survival of indigenous language, cultures and visions. It is essential to promote intercultural education in order to sensitize indigenous and non-indigenous children and youth to each other's cultural value systems.

10. Link local and national advocacy work for the promotion of indigenous rights to the global level, and link global work to the national and local.

The linkages between the local and the global and vice-versa have to be strengthened so that the problems at the local and national levels will be better communicated to and understood by the international community. Issues faced by indigenous peoples at the local and national levels should inform decisions, programmes and priorities of global institutions. In the same vein, the awareness of indigenous peoples on global developments should be raised and steps to mitigate actual and potential adverse impacts should be taken. The gains achieved at the international level, especially in terms of the creation of spaces, processes and mechanisms that promote indigenous rights and development must be disseminated widely so that these can be effectively used.

10.1. Undertake education and training activities for indigenous peoples to become more aware of national and global developments. Build their capacities to occupy, engage and use more effectively existing spaces, mechanisms and processes to raise their issues and concerns. Seek redress for their complaints and get national and global institutions to be more responsive and sensitive to indigenous situations and perspectives.

10.2. Facilitate effective participation of indigenous representatives to global and regional processes (i.e. UN Permanent Forum on Indigenous Issues, Commission on Human Rights, Working Group on Indigenous Populations, Organization of American States, Draft Declaration process, etc.). Geographical, gender and intergenerational balance should be ensured in choosing potential participants.

5

10.3. Encourage and support efforts of indigenous participants to disseminate more widely what they have learned in the various global processes, so that awareness on global developments will be raised and inter-linkages between local and global issues are better understood and established.

10.4. Facilitate networking among indigenous peoples. Enhance possibilities for undertaking joint activities and campaigns among them for better impact.

10.5. Develop innovative partnerships between indigenous organizations and UN bodies, agencies, programmes and funds towards developing and implementing more programmes and projects promoting indigenous rights and development.

11. Strengthen indigenous governance systems and capacities of indigenous peoples to govern and influence decision-making processes, mechanisms and policy development.

Modern nation-state building has undermined many indigenous governance systems. Fortunately, in many communities, indigenous systems still co-exist with modern systems. There is a need to strengthen these systems and enhance their best elements and features such as consensual decision-making processes, promotion of the collective good, responsibility, mutual support and accountability, among others. The weaknesses of indigenous governance systems, such as discrimination against women and other democratic deficits, etc. must also be addressed.

11.1. Analyse how national and local governance systems undermine or reinforce indigenous governance systems and customary laws. Make recommendations on how to interface these two systems so that indigenous rights and development will be enhanced.

11.2. Help develop training programmes and institutes for indigenous parliamentarians and indigenous civil servants to increase capabilities, especially in terms of ensuring that the indigenous peoples' agenda for rights and development are integrated into their work.

11.3. Facilitate exchange visits between indigenous parliamentarians and between representatives of indigenous governments to learn more about each other's situations and experiences in governance.

11.4. Enhance capacities of indigenous peoples to influence decisions and decision-making processes in government and intergovernmental bodies. Ensure that they are effectively participating at all stages of decision-making in programmes, policies and institutions doing development work.

11.5. Undertake awareness and capacity-building training workshops for government bureaucrats and politicians so that they will become more sensitive and responsive to indigenous rights and development.

12. Strengthen the roles of indigenous leaders, traditional authorities and indigenous women in resolving and mediating conflict issues.

Several conflict situations in indigenous peoples' territories still remain unresolved. Even in areas where armed struggle has stopped and peace negotiations took place, there is still a lot of dissatisfaction in the implementation of negotiated peace agreements. There is a need to analyse why this is so and to develop innovative steps to address these situations more satisfactorily. The role of traditional authorities, indigenous leaders, and indigenous women in conflict resolution and mediation should be enhanced. Lessons learned in helping resolve or transform conflicts should be shared and discussed in more detail.

6

Workshop Report: Indigenous Peoples' Rights and Development – Engaging in Dialogue

I. Introduction

For the Asia-Pacific region, the most relevant international financial institutions are the Asian Development Bank (ADB), the Japan Bank for International Cooperation (JBIC) and the World Bank (WB). Projects developed and implemented by these institutions impact enormously on the rights and livelihoods of indigenous peoples throughout the region. In recognition of this, WB and ADB have developed policies and guidelines for project development and funding in the territories and lands of indigenous peoples. However, consultations with indigenous peoples have demonstrated that there remain significant concerns with the policies as they currently stand, and that there are varying levels of knowledge regarding the policies both within the institutions themselves and among indigenous peoples. In addition, there has been some movement within the institutions themselves towards policy review, complemented by a willingness to engage with indigenous peoples in reviewing these policies. To this end, sustained engagement and education of indigenous peoples' organizations in the development policies and interventions of international financial agencies is essential for full and effective participation in these processes.

In response to the opportunity and need to create stronger and more effective dialogue between indigenous peoples and the international financial institutions active in the region, UNDP-RIPP (Regional Initiative on Indigenous Peoples' Rights and Development) and DINTEG (The Cordillera Peoples Legal Centre) held a planning workshop to strategize on how best to both increase indigenous capacities in engaging the international financial institutions (IFIs) and create a space for policy dialogue with the same. This initiative was developed in response to a request to RIPP by indigenous participants at the UN Permanent Forum on Indigenous Issues (May 2005) to facilitate a process of dialogue with IFIs active in the Asia-Pacific region. This report covers the process and outcome of that planning workshop conducted on 4-6 November 2005 in Baguio City, Cordillera, Philippines.

The planning workshop involved indigenous leaders and representatives from throughout Asia; members of the UN Permanent Forum on indigenous Issues (PFII); ADB and UNDP. The workshop was hosted and organized by the Cordillera Indigenous Peoples' Legal Centre (DINTEG) in partnership and with the support of UNDP-RIPP Regional Centre in Bangkok.

The key objectives of the workshop were:

1. To initiate a process of dialogue between indigenous peoples and IFIs;

2. To provide a forum in which key indigenous leaders in the region can discuss and agree strategies of engagement with IFIs;

3. To conduct a gap analysis on knowledge and capacity on the polices and programmes of IFIs with regard to indigenous peoples;

4. To finalize the content, methodology and time-frame for the dialogue process complemented by a training programme on the Human Rights Based Approach;

5. To establish a core group to function as the 'planning committee' to provide guidance and leadership in the training process and ensure wide consultation; and

6. To build the capacity of indigenous peoples' organizations and communities in protecting their rights and determining their own development.

6

II. Framework

Strategic planning and preparation for the proposed training events on IFIs in Asia was the focus of the workshop. However before entering the strategic planning sessions, relevant inputs to provide the general framework within which the proposed training programme is to be situated were shared by experts.

Ms. Chandra Roy, Programme Coordinator of the UNDP-RIPP, provided an overview of UNDP's strategic objectives and the UN Common Understanding on a Human Rights-Based Approach (HRBA) to Development, a policy advocating for a development strategy that places advancement of human rights as both a goal and methodological approach. She also elaborated on UNDP's policy of engagement with indigenous peoples (2001) and the work and outreach of RIPP.

Greater elaboration was provided by Robert Bernardo from the UNDP Capacity 2015 Programme, Asia Region, which is currently working on a resource guide on capacity assessment and development using the HRBA perspective. Noteworthy to mention is the on-going initiative of Capacity 2015 to design an complex but straightforward assessment instrument on institutional performance related to leadership, external relations, programme planning, monitoring and evaluation, external relations and sustainability.

The indigenous perspective of the use of the HRBA and the operationalization of this approach was provided by Victoria Tauli-Corpus, Chair of the United Nations Permanent Forum on Indigenous Issues. This was supported and extended by a presentation on the contentious issue of free, prior and informed consent by Parshuram Tamang, Asia member of the UNPFII. Both emphasized that at the centre of a rights-based approach to development for indigenous peoples is respecting, promoting, protecting and fulfilling the right to self-determination of which one illustrative manifestation is the right to free, prior and informed consent. From the perspective of indigenous peoples, a policy or intervention will be judged as "development" in so far as it will promote and fulfil the right to self determination, by which one concrete application is if the development intervention will uphold the right to free, prior and informed consent.

The challenge is the operationalization of the HRBA in a manner consistent with the interests, needs and perspective of indigenous peoples with specific interest in engaging IFIs such as the World Bank Group (WBG), ADB and JBIC – the three major banks influencing development in Asia.

To provide an understanding on the policies of IFIs impacting on indigenous peoples' lands and territories in Asia, three case studies were presented:

World Bank Group: A comprehensive review on the WBG's policy on indigenous peoples and its application at the project level was presented by Ms. Vicky Tauli-Corpuz, together with concluding recommendations for engagement of the WBG by indigenous peoples. Both positive efforts of WBG at engagement in the past, and weaknesses seen in that engagement process, were presented for participants and discussed.[1]

---

[1] The background paper on the World Bank Group was prepared by Fergus McKay, who was unable to participate at the workshop. Representatives of the World Bank were also unable to participate, but have indicated their interest in the dialogue.

Asian Development Bank: Ms. Indira Simbolon, with support from Mr. Albab Akanda, presented the ADB's current policy on indigenous peoples, and provided some details on the review process currently being undertaken by ADB on the indigenous peoples' policy, and two other social and environmental responsibility policies. The presentation detailed the purpose of the policy: to promote effective participation, to mitigate adverse impacts and to provide information to indigenous peoples and to the public. The review process is referred to as the 'safeguard policy update' and is intended to enhance flexibility of ADB's work and contribute to the achievement of the Millennium Development Goals (MDGs).

A review of the ADB's policy from an indigenous perspective was provided by Raja Devasish Roy from the Chittagong Hill Tracts. Both weaknesses and positive features of the policy were elaborated on with concluding recommendations on reforming the current policy towards "unequivocal commitment to honour and respect" the rights of indigenous peoples. Further, it was firmly recommended that the review process should be designed and implemented together with indigenous peoples representatives and that the process should not repeat the policy review process of WBG which was viewed as insufficient at best, and resulted in a weakened policy on the protection of the rights of indigenous peoples.

Japan Bank of International Cooperation: The third case study was on JBIC, the second largest 'development' bank in the world with 80 percent of its loans directed to Asia. In contrast to the ADB and WBG, JBIC does not have a policy specially designed for indigenous peoples. However, it has recently established environmental and social guidelines that are relevant to indigenous peoples, with certain provisions specific to indigenous peoples. The issues paper was prepared by Joan Carling of the Cordillera Peoples Alliance and Hozue Hatae of the Friends of the Earth-Japan. Ms. Carling presented the paper and elaborated as examples four cases of indigenous peoples' engagement with JBIC: Kotong Panjang Dam in Indonesia; San Roque Dam in the Philippines; Kelau Dam in Malaysia; and Sakhalin II Oil Development Project in Russia. The four case studies illustrated the lack of respect for indigenous peoples' rights by the JBIC, and its failure to conform to its own policies.

From these three case studies of banks, a ten-point comparative observation was drawn, which includes but is not limited to the following:

- The overriding concern of the safeguard policies of the three banks are mitigation of adverse impact on the environment and social cost among indigenous peoples.

- Both WB and ADB have specific policy safeguards pertaining to indigenous peoples. JBIC has no specific policy on indigenous peoples but has a specific provision pertaining to indigenous peoples in its policy on environmental and social responsibility.

- All three banks have provisions on mandatory safeguards to mitigate social and environmental impact, although these differ in extent and coverage.

- All three banks uphold mandatory provisions on mitigation of adverse impacts.

- All three banks have specific policies on involuntary resettlement/physical relocation with particular concern on avoidance if possible and if not, at least with varying structured processes of support and participation from affected communities.

- All three banks have explicit provisions for information disclosure. The policies and procedures however, remain inadequate.

6

- All three banks maintain mechanisms for appeals and accountability. The mechanisms though are faulty and bureaucratic with no effective mechanisms to seek redress and justice. Further, there is no clear application of appeals and accountability in relation to WBG's policy on "free, prior and informed consultation leading to broad support."

III. Proposed actions and time frame

Being fully convinced of the impact of powerful international financial institutions on indigenous peoples and recognizing the gap in the capacity of indigenous peoples to deal with these institutions, the participants agreed to address such need through a supplementary training programme. The immediate goal is to produce training manuals with subsequent training activities to be organized at sub-regional and national levels.

Three separate working group discussions took place during the workshop dealing with the three identified sections of the training manual. Each working group discussed surveying capacity needs, target groups, methodologies of delivery, content, existing manuals on similar topics and strategic approaches to the provision of such training and its overall objectives. The three modules that were discussed and which emerged from the plenary discussion of the presentations from the working groups were:

1. Volume I 'Human Rights and Emerging Standards on Indigenous Rights': will focus on frameworks on human rights and indigenous peoples rights, which include: the Convention concerning Indigenous and Tribal Peoples in Independent Countries (ILO No. 169); Convention on the Elimination of All Forms of Discrimination against Women (CEDAW); Convention on the Rights of the Child (CRC); International Covenant on Economic, Social and Cultural Rights (ICESCR); International Covenant on Civil and Political Rights (ICCPR), and the Millennium Declaration and Millennium Development Goals, among others.

2. Volume II 'Human Rights-Based Approaches, Uses and Advocacy': will focus on operationalizing the human rights-based approach to development and advocacy work that will strike on free, prior and informed consent principles and approaches.

3. Volume III 'Development Financing Agencies': will focus on International Financial Agencies, their policies and their approaches to and strategies of engagement related to indigenous peoples.

Details of the presentations from each of the working groups was then provided for a plenary session during which all participants worked together to produce a combined plan for the training module and the three volumes within it.

Following the establishment of the draft outline of the desired training manual and sub-volumes, the workshop brainstormed on the concrete 'next steps' and commitments through which the training manual will be developed. A tabulated summary of these next steps is presented in Table 1.

6

Table 1: Summary of next steps for training manual development

Consolidation of framework

Review outputs of workshop

Semi-finalize objectives for each volume, target and module/submodule

Establish HRBA/IP CD Task Force: Rhoda Dalang; Joan Carling; Victoria Tauli-Corpuz; Parshuram Tamang; Raja Devasish Roy; Roy Laifungbam, Rukka Sombolinggi and RIPP

Volume 1: South Asia Regional Office of the IAITPTF – Parshuram Tamang

Volume 2: Tebtebba Foundation – Victoria Tauli-Corpuz

Volume 3: CPA – Joan Carling

Mapping and inventory

Electronic mapping/survey and capacity assessment

"Best practice" compilation and consolidation

Compilation of reference materials/documents, case studies (including existing kits/guides)

Finalization of framework for training manual development

Review and prioritize capacity gaps to be addressed by training manual (Workshop 1, TF + key resource persons)

Finalize objectives for each volume, targets, and modules/submodules (Workshop 1)

Electronic process of validation of consolidated framework

Identify training/CD methodologies for each module/submodule

Content development

Assignment (volunteering) of individuals to follow-up specific modules

Writing of modules

Review and consolidation of training modules (Workshop 1)

Editing and publication of manuals

Two sub-regional trainings: South Asia and South-East Asia

20 participants in each workshop

Training of trainers for national application

While RIPP-UNDP and DINTEG will take the lead in the whole project, the task force identified above was created to collaborate on keeping on track with the plan to proceed as envisioned. Being fully aware of related initiatives in training and module development by other organizations and agencies, each task force is will to coordinate and work collaboratively with these groups.

All three volumes of the training manual are expected to be available for piloting in sub-regional trainings, one set for South Asia and another set for South-East Asia. Each training will target 20 participants. It will be during these sub-regional trainings that the plan for subsequent national trainings will be detailed. These national trainings are set to take off by the year 2007.

6

Annex

Salient Features of Policies on Indigenous Peoples of
the World Bank Group and Asian Development Bank,
and Major Concerns of Indigenous Peoples

Table 2: Summary of policies of WBG and ADB on indigenous peoples

Features	WBG (*OP4.10/BP4. 10 July 2005*)	ADB (*Policy on Indigenous Peoples, April 1998*)	Major concerns of indigenous peoples
A. Working definition of indigenous peoples	A.1. Characteristics: ■ Self-identification …and recognition of this identity by others ■ Collective attachment to geographically distinct habitats or ancestral territories …and to the natural resources in these habitats and territories ■ Customary cultural, economic, social, or political institutions that are separate from those of the dominant society and culture ■ An indigenous language… A.2. WBG requires "technical judgment" to ascertain groups considered as indigenous peoples	A.1. Two major characteristics: ■ Descent from population groups… most often before modern states were created and before modern borders were defined ■ Maintenance of cultural and social identities, and social and economic, cultural and political institutions separate from mainstream or dominant societies and cultures A.2. Additional characteristics: ■ Self-identification and identification by others as being part of a distinct indigenous cultural group… ■ A linguistic identity different from that of the dominant society ■ Social, cultural, economic and political traditions and institutions distinct from the dominant culture ■ Economic systems oriented more toward traditional systems of production than mainstream systems ■ Unique ties and attachments to traditional habitats and ancestral territories and natural resources in these habitats and territories	■ Self-identification and identification by others is a positive element but not as primary criterion ■ Avoidance to reference on historical continuity to ancestral territories and natural resources ■ Avoidance on reference to ownership to ancestral land/ territories/natural resources ■ WBG's reliance on "technical judgment" ■ WBG and ADB's reference to domestic law/policy related to identification of indigenous peoples

Table 2: Summary of policies of WBG and ADB on indigenous peoples (continued)

Features	WBG (*OP4.10/BP4. 10 July 2005*)	ADB (*Policy on Indigenous Peoples, April 1998*)	Major concerns of indigenous peoples
B. Policy framework	B.1. Indigenous peoples: ■ Among the most marginalized and vulnerable segments of the population ■ Identities and cultures inextricably linked to the lands on which they live and natural resources on which they depend ■ Economic, social, legal status often limits their capacity to defend their interests in and rights to lands, territories… and/ or restricts their ability to participate in and benefit from development ■ Play vital role in sustainable development	B.1. Indigenous peoples regarded as: ■ One of the largest vulnerable segments of society ■ Disadvantaged in terms of social indicators, economic status and quality of life ■ Not able to participate equally in development processes and share in the benefits of development Lack of participation of indigenous peoples in development combined with the loss of access to land and resources have in many cases marginalized indigenous peoples	

Table 2: Summary of policies of WBG and ADB on indigenous peoples (continued)

Features	WBG (*OP4.10/BP4. 10 July 2005*)	ADB (*Policy on Indigenous Peoples, April 1998*)	Major concerns of indigenous peoples
C. Policy objectives	■ Contributes to WBG's mission of poverty reduction and sustainable development by ensuring that the development process fully respects the dignity, human rights, economies and cultures of indigenous peoples	■ Ensure that indigenous peoples have opportunities to participate in and benefit equally from development ■ Avoid negatively affecting indigenous peoples ■ Provide adequate and appropriate compensation when negative impact is unavoidable ■ Ensure that initiatives should be conceived, planned, and implemented, to the maximum extent possible, with the informed consent of affected communities and include respect for indigenous peoples' dignity, human rights and cultural uniqueness ■ Policy on indigenous peoples would be complemented and supported by, other bank policies. ...not to obviate the requirement of compliance with other ADB policies	

Table 2: Summary of policies of WBG and ADB on indigenous peoples (continued)

Features	WBG (*OP4.10/BP4. 10 July 2005*)	ADB (*Policy on Indigenous Peoples, April 1998*)	Major concerns of indigenous peoples
D. Policy elements	■ WBG requires the borrower to engage in a process of free, prior and informed consultation… resulting to broad community support ■ Measures to avoid potentially adverse effects on indigenous peoples' communities or when avoidance is not feasible, minimize, mitigate or compensate for such effects ■ Ensure that indigenous peoples receive social and economic benefits that are culturally appropriate and gender and intergenerational inclusive	Policy must ensure that interventions are: ■ Consistent with the needs and aspirations of affected indigenous peoples ■ Compatible in substance and structure with affected indigenous peoples' culture and social and economic institutions ■ Conceived, planned and implemented with the informed participation of affected communities ■ Equitable in terms of development efforts and impact ■ Not imposing the negative effects of development without appropriate and acceptable compensation	■ *Free Prior Informed Consultation (FPICon)* is weak in safeguarding interests and rights of indigenous peoples. Policy must provide for free, prior and informed consent ■ ADB's informed participation is a higher standard than WBG's FPICon ■ Non-inclusion of recognition and protection of territorial rights and right to self-determination ■ No outright prohibition of involuntary resettlement
E. Scope of applicability	OP4.10 (July 2005) is applicable to public sector arm of WBG. For private sector, Performance Standard 7 (date) is WBG's policy guideline	Policy applicable to both the public and private sectors	■ Should not the private and public sector deal with indigenous peoples with equal standards?

Table 2: Summary of policies of WBG and ADB on indigenous peoples (continued)

Features	WBG (*OP4.10/BP4. 10 July 2005*)	ADB (*Policy on Indigenous Peoples, April 1998*)	Major concerns of indigenous peoples
F. Operational processes	F.1. **Screening** by the WBG to determine whether indigenous peoples are present or have collective attachment to the project area. WBG seeks technical judgment of qualified social scientists. WBG consults with indigenous peoples concerned and the borrower F.2. **Social Assessment** conducted by borrower through social scientists acceptable to the WBG: ■ To evaluate potential positive and adverse effects… and examine project alternatives where adverse effects may be significant. ■ Breadth, depth, and type of analysis are proportional to the nature and scale of project's potential effects on indigenous peoples F.2.1. Where the project affects indigenous peoples, the borrower engages in free, prior and informed consultation with them F.2.2. Borrower ascertains free, prior and informed consultation resulting to broad support from representatives of major sections of the community (footnote-BP4.10 para 7). F.2.3. WBG reviews the process and the outcome of the consultation carried out by the borrower.	F.1. **Initial Social Assessment** ■ Undertaken during project preparatory technical assistance fact-finding ■ Identifies indigenous peoples affected significantly: needs, demands, capacities, other social dimensions F.2. **Indigenous Peoples Development Plan (IPDP)** ■ IPDP must be prepared if indigenous peoples are likely to be affected significantly (if they positively or negatively (i) affect their customary rights of use and access to land and natural resources; (ii) change their socioeconomic status; (iii) affect their cultural and communal integrity; (iv) affect their health, education, livelihood, and/or social security status; and/or (v) alter or undermine the recognition of indigenous knowledge) ■ Takes into full account desires and preferred options of affected indigenous peoples ■ Identify adverse effects and measures to avoid, mitigate or compensate for these adverse effects	■ High probability of underestimated and mischaracterized impacts; probability of focusing on economic impacts ■ Non-inclusion of affected indigenous peoples in the operational processes from social assessment to formulation of development plans/ frameworks. They will only be consulted ■ Broad community support not required for IPP/IPPF in OP4.10, however, BP4.10 requires broad community support from representatives of major sections of the community ■ No clear indicators for broad community support; indigenous peoples excluded in assessing whether broad community support exists; collective decision-making processes and structures of indigenous peoples stand to be undermined

Table 2: Summary of policies of WBG and ADB on indigenous peoples (continued)

Features	WBG (*OP4.10/BP4. 10 July 2005*)	ADB (*Policy on Indigenous Peoples, April 1998*)	Major concerns of indigenous peoples
	F.3. **Indigenous Peoples Plan/Planning Framework (IPP/IPPF)** F.3.1. **IPP** sets out measures to ensure that: ■ Indigenous peoples affected by the project receive culturally appropriate social and economic benefits; and ■ When potential adverse effects are identified, those adverse effects are avoided, minimized, mitigated, or compensated for F.3.2. **IPPF** is prepared by the borrower when indigenous peoples are likely to be present in, or have collective attachment but can't be determined until the programme or subprojects are identified F.4. **Disclosure of IPP/IPPF** ■ The borrower makes the social assessment and draft IPP/IPPF available to affected indigenous peoples' communities in an appropriate form, manner and language ■ WBG makes them available to the public and again to indigenous peoples in accordance with *The World Bank Policy on Disclosure of Information*	■ Involvement of appropriate existing institutions, local organizations and NGOs… ■ Capacity building for indigenous peoples… to effective participation in development processes ■ IPDP is the responsibility of the government or project sponsor ■ IPDP must be acceptable to ADB F.3. It is necessary that ADB integrates concern for indigenous peoples into each step of the programming project processing and policy development cycles F.4. **Disclosure**: ■ Effective approaches to information dissemination and communication with indigenous peoples communities should be identified	

Table 2: Summary of policies of WBG and ADB on indigenous peoples (continued)

Features	WBG (*OP4.10/BP4. 10 July 2005*)	ADB (*Policy on Indigenous Peoples, April 1998*)	Major concerns of indigenous peoples
G. Monitoring, evaluation and accountability	■ Operations Evaluation Department is responsible for monitoring and evaluating compliance as well as accountability with the Inspection Panel mandated to investigate complaints	■ Office of Environment and Social Development together with the Programmes Department resident missions in the countries and the Operations Evaluation Office are mandated for the task of monitoring and evaluation of compliance to the policies ■ The policy requires that indigenous peoples issues be addressed in the monitoring and evaluation processes and that indigenous peoples participate in these processes	■ Lack of indicators for IP participation ■ Lack of clearer guidelines on accountability and effective grievance mechanisms ■ No built-in grievance/ complaints/ mediation mechanism for addressing disputes relating to existence of broad community support

The Banks' (WBG and ADB) policies as presented in Table 2 focus largely on safeguarding the environment and indigenous peoples from the adverse impacts of the Banks' interventions. To address these major concerns, the Banks have put in place a number of affirmative principles, policies and approaches that indigenous peoples could invoke as they continue to pursue for policy reforms.

Both Banks enforce mandatory observance of the right of indigenous peoples to participation, mitigation of adverse impact and compensation. Further, the Banks require borrowers to conduct Social Assessment/Initial Social Assessment, meaningful consultation with affected indigenous peoples, preparation of an Indigenous Peoples Plan (IPP) for WBG and Indigenous Peoples Development Plan (IPDP) for ADB. The Initial Social Assessment of ADB and Screening and Social Assessment of WBG elaborate the operational processes of the Banks to assess possible negative impacts. It is from the Social Assessment and Initial Social Assessment that the IPDP for the ADB and IPP/IPPF for WB will be mapped out. IPDP/ IPP/IPPF would further "form a basis for project implementation and for monitoring and evaluation of how the project deals with IP issues".

Alongside these affirmative policies, however, the Banks' policies do not include affected communities in conducting their Social Assessment and in the formulation of Indigenous Peoples Development Plan (IPDP). It should be noted further that the application of impact assessments and corresponding "development" plans rests on the "type, location, scale, nature and magnitude" of the "potential effects" on indigenous peoples. These can undermine the affirmative provisions accorded under the relevant policies.

The Japan Bank for International Cooperation (JBIC) has no specific safeguard policy pertaining to indigenous peoples. However, in the *Guidelines for Confirmation of Environmental and Social Considerations* (April 2002), the sole provision specifically pertaining to indigenous peoples quoted below, provides a clearer perspective on land rights:

> *When a project may have adverse impact on indigenous peoples, all of their rights in relation to land and resources must be respected in accordance with the spirit of the relevant international declarations and treaties. Efforts must be made to obtain the consent of indigenous peoples after they have been fully informed. (footnote)*

It is worthy to acknowledge this affirmative provision of JBIC with respect to land and resource rights which is with reference to international declarations and treaties. Equally important to underscore is the absence of linking the JBIC policy with domestic laws and policies which could be theoretically advantageous to indigenous peoples. However, JBIC does not require project proponents to obtain free and prior consent of indigenous peoples, but only to make efforts to do so after indigenous peoples have been fully informed of project impacts.

Indigenous peoples all over the world have been asserting that at the crux of their development in all spheres – economic, social, cultural and political – is the recognition of their inherent right to their lands, territories and resources and the right to self-determination. For the indigenous peoples, development means liberation from centuries of exploitation of their resources and liberation from discrimination and oppression. Recognizing the right to ancestral lands, territories and the right to self-determination will pave the way towards the full realization of human dignity both as individuals and as collectivities. These are the major concerns with which indigenous peoples would like to be incorporated in Safeguard Policies if these are to fully protect the interests and rights of indigenous peoples.

About the authors

Friends of the Earth-Japan (FoE Japan) is an international NGO that deals with environmental problems at the global level. Members of Friends of the Earth International have been working in Japan since 1980 and specialize in the issues of global warming, deforestations and development aid.

Jill Cariño represents the Cordillera Women's Education and Resource Centre (CWERC) in the Philippines.

Joan Carling is Chairperson of the Cordillera Peoples' Alliance (CPA) in the Philippines.

Rhoda Dalang represents the Cordillera Indigenous Peoples' Legal Centre (DINTEG).

Fergus Mackay is Coordinator of the Legal and Human Rights Programme, Forest Peoples' Programme.

Raja Devasish Roy is Chakma Chief of the Chittagong Hill Tracts region in Bangladesh. He is a lawyer (barrister) by training and has practiced law in Dhaka since 1988, including in the Supreme Court of Bangladesh. He is also associated with several voluntary organizations within Bangladesh involved with human rights, indigenous peoples' rights, research and development.

Victoria Tauli-Corpuz is Chairperson of the United Nations Permanent Forum on Indigenous Issues (PFII), Executive Director of Tebtebba (Indigenous Peoples' International Centre for Policy Research and Education), and Convenor of the Asian Indigenous Women's Network (AIWN).